D1085047

MEDIEVAL PARIS
The Town of Books

by

MILDRED PRIÇA BJERKEN

The Scarecrow Press, Inc.
Metuchen, N.J.   1973

Library of Congress Cataloging in Publication Data

Bjerken, Mildred Priça.
  Medieval Paris, the town of books.

  Bibliography: p.
  1. Books--History--Paris. 2. Paris--Libraries--
History. 3. Paris--Intellectual life. I. Title.
Z8.F82P33   914.4'36'032   73-1903
ISBN 0-8108-0600-2

To
my son
Ray

PREFACE

This study represents an anthropological approach to the role of the library as a social institution. It is one section of a larger work intended as a thesis whose purpose was to provide an historical view of the library through the medium of the printed book and its precursors, focusing upon their cultural relationship to cities. The subject of the proposed thesis was tantalizingly complex and tempted me by its fascination to go on and on until the study became too long. The theme of this section on Paris is that the city of Paris having adequately performed its cultural role as a university city, that of enlarging and transmitting a complex culture from generation to generation, the volume of book production was increased, which left its physical mark upon the face of the city and brought about an expansion of the physical boundaries of the city.

To relate the library to the city is to relate it to a great social movement in space and time. Urbanization is one of the social forces which is currently effecting dramatic changes. The march of urban growth has forced upon people the study of the city in all its manifestations, from the sociological aspects of racial tensions to the creation of "bedroom cities" where people return when the day's work is done, to regional planning all over the world. Material on the cities is also material on the sources and springs of civilizations since cities were the carriers of civilization and culture. As civilizations reached their prime, libraries developed. Closely related to this is the effect of cities upon man himself, for the city is people. Medieval Paris, then, is a study of "the town of books," as it was called by Pope Gregory IX in the thirteenth century, and of its people. Although the emphasis is upon book production, every factor of that process has its reflex action in the library, and it is hoped that this work will add in some way to the public esteem of the library, public esteem being important because of the library's dependence upon public support for financial assistance.

This work is inevitably and unavoidably dependent

upon the work of others and I cannot claim any originality for it; everything has been said before; only the knot which binds the various threads together do I claim as my own. I have tried to give full credit for all the works consulted, and their titles appear in the bibliography.

I would like to express my indebtedness to the teaching of Professors Clarence J. Glacken, Eugene Hammel, and Thomas C. Patterson of the University of California at Berkeley, whose courses on the urban landscape and culture growth gave me a new awareness of the relationships between cities and people and things. In addition I offer my gratitude and sincere appreciation to those who have given help and encouragement and their precious time: Mrs. Jean E. Wichers and Mr. Leslie H. Janke of the Department of Librarianship, California State University at San Jose; Mr. William Kirkwood, Orange County Public Library; Mrs. Adella Robinson of the Inter-Library Loan Department at the Santa Ana Public Library and the librarians of the University of California at Santa Barbara, who made long-sought volumes available.

Mildred Bjerken

CONTENTS

INTRODUCTION

The city of Paris owed its pre-eminence in the Middle Ages to cultural and political causes. Both the cultural development and the political history of Paris were in turn influenced by its geographical situation and topographical characteristics. No view of the historical process based exclusively upon an economic interpretation of the past, according to Douglas, suffices to explain the luster or the unique prestige of medieval Paris during its Golden Age, the period extending roughly from 1125 to 1300.[1] Nor does it explain the power of attraction or the influence Paris had over the mind and the imagination of European men. Paris was a capital city: capital city of France, capital city of Western Europe, capital city of Christendom. To Parisians, Paris was also the capital city of charm. A tapestry now in Beauvais Cathedral pays homage to the legendary Paris, son of Troy's King Priam, who, setting beauty above power and intellect, awarded the golden apple to Venus. It was only natural, then, Parisians claim, for this prince of love to found on the banks of the Seine the capital city of charm.[2] In its Golden Age another prince, Abelard, the prince of free-lance teachers, was to launch Paris on a new course as a university city which would earn for it the title of intellectual capital of Europe.

The four cardinal institutions which contributed to the greatness of medieval Paris were Monarchy, Church, Bourgeoisie, University. After the preceding centuries of flux, politically chaotic and groping toward integration, Paris, by the thirteenth century, had reached a confident equilibrium. The city of Paris united its various activities in relation to a common purpose and, royal capital of a nation which itself had been consolidated into one unit, it also became the cultural and intellectual capital of Europe and the ecclesiastical capital of Christendom.

Medieval Paris was the largest city of transalpine Europe and the vital center of that universe. Symbolic of its status is the brass compass star set in the pavement in the square in front of Notre Dame Cathedral, Kilomètre

1

Zéro; all distances are measured from this point in the middle of the island in the middle of the river in the middle of
the city. This is the center of things; everything begins
from here.[3] Every road in France centers inwardly on the
cathedral; one may start walking to Notre Dame on the green
roads of Normandy or on the sun-drenched roads of Provence. Medieval civilization was essentially a French creation, and Paris was the center upon which the creative forces
of France and of Europe converged.[4]

    Although it is not located in the geographical center of
France, Paris does occupy a key position in that country's
network of communications. Lines of communication have
played an essential role in the cultural growth of Paris, for
along them ideas, customs, and influences found their way to
be cross-fertilized within the city. Paris provided an ideal
setting for a flourishing culture. Here medieval art and
thought reached their zenith. The harmonious balance of
dominant cultural forces in the thirteenth century, by their
combined action on a single city, made medieval Paris the
capital of European civilization.[5] Insofar as the cultural
achievement of the Middle Ages was based upon a classical
tradition modified by the teaching of the Church, Douglas
says, to this extent medieval Paris was representative of
that civilization at the climax of its development.[6] Monarchy
or Church would not of themselves have assured for Paris
its unique position at the center of medieval Europe, as
Douglas has pointed out, but Paris alone among the cities of
Western Europe was a university city, and its university was
the prototype of nearly all the later ones of transalpine
Europe.[7] Paris was a university city before it had a university.

    The roots of the nation's prime institutions are deep
in other ages. After an introductory discussion of the historical background of these forces pulsating through medieval
Paris, the interaction of which contributed to the development
of Paris in the thirteenth century as a university city, the
discussion in this volume continues with the development of
mercantile, royal, ecclesiastical, and university quarters
within the city and the contribution, through the translation
of the function of each sector into its dominant structure, to
the design of the city. Mumford's definitive work on the
city in history provided most of the necessary concepts upon
which the material herein on the function of the city is
based.[8]

    The purpose of this study is to show the cultural

relationship between Paris, the university city, and book production before and after the introduction of printing into
Paris. The discussion then continues with the growth of the
University of Paris and the development of its organization;
with teaching methods, the main thrust of which is the scientific method, and the role of printing in the development
of that method; with the production of books, and the effect
of the growth in volume upon the physical expansion of the
city of Paris. To avoid an overlapping of facts, the synthesis is presented in terms of people and the summary is presented within the context of the reign of Francis I, which
method summarizes the subjects discussed by presenting
them within a different context. The limit of the time period is specified as the close of the sixteenth century, although
it was found convenient at certain points to make reference
to events of a somewhat later date in order to show the developing trend of events.

* * *

Paris had not always been a capital city. A capital
city in the political sense is one which has been made a seat
of government for the convenience of a state that is greater
than is its capital, implying that a state which is governed
from a capital city would include other cities besides the
capital and other rural areas besides the one from which the
capital draws its food supply. The city to be selected as the
seat of government must meet three criteria, according to
Toynbee: it must be a location convenient for serving as an
administrative center for the whole country, a location within easy reach of abundant sources of food for supplying a
large urban population, and a location that will be a good
strategic center for defending the country's frontiers. [9] The
site of Paris met all three criteria: Paris was a good administrative center; it was a city that could easily be provisioned because of its location at a key point in the basin
of the Seine River; and it was also relatively close to the
northeastern frontier of France, which was its most vul-
nerable area.

Paris, situated on the Ile de la Cité, which is chief
of the three islands in the Seine, grew up at the intersection of two great natural highways. One of these was the
river Seine itself, which divides into two arms around the
Ile de la Cité. Located in midstream, Paris spans the
Seine just below the confluence of the Marne and the Oise
with that river. Three navigable waterways thus converge
upon Paris. [10] The other natural highway was the land

route leading from the Rhine district to the south by way of
what later became the Rue Saint-Martin on the right bank of
the Seine and the Rue Saint-Jacques on the left bank. This
land route crossed the Seine at the point where it was most
easily forded, the Ile de la Cité.[11] Paris was thus a crossroads rather than a terminus. The road and the river
crossed east and west, north and south; from Champagne to
England, from Flanders to Provence. Dozens of secondary
roads and streams also led to the city from every point on
the horizon. The Romans had recognized the importance of
this site, making "Lutetia," as their Paris was then called,
the center of a road system.[12]

        Paris thus developed on the natural stronghold of an
island, girdled by the branches of the Seine. The original
island was about half the size of the modern Ile de la Cité
and was subjected to flooding by the river. This site was
not, therefore, a normal one for a town and could only have
been selected for defensive reasons. For about two thousand
years the Seine had been the city's defensive moat and its
main highway.[13]

        What has happened on the banks of the Seine through
the centuries has profoundly affected both the history and
the character of the city and the character of its people.
The stories and the lore about the river and its history were
handed down through the ages by oral tradition and became
woven into legends. Legends of a river goddess remained
alive in human memories to find visual representation in
later centuries. The Seine was known to the ancient Gauls
as the Sequan, and they acknowledged a river goddess,
Sequana, to whom they built a temple at the source of the
river which traced her remembered shape more than one
hundred and fifty miles away. Today, a temple stands
there, built by the city of Paris. Although the Seine is almost five hundred miles long, winding its way from the
hills of Burgundy down to the Channel at Le Havre, the
river achieves its true status for Parisians only within the
gates of the city. The Parisian city fathers had bought the
square kilometer around the source of the river at Saint
Germain-la-Fouille, where the waters bubble up into a man-
made grotto and eddy about the statue of a recumbent
woman.[14]

        The continuity of ancient tradition is manifested in
the seal of the city of Paris. A ship or barque with the
motto Fluctuat nec mergitur, "It rides the waves and does

not sink, " was the seal of the <u>Nautes de Paris</u> before the
Romans came, and gradually it became the seal of the city.[15]
The members of this company of water merchants had dedicated an altar to Jupiter in the city of Paris. [16]   The sym-
bolism of the barque recognizes the importance of the river
in the life of the city.

The topographical characteristics of the city's surroundings influenced its early development.   To the south,
although the relief of the hills was moderate, these hills approached close to the river.   This fact tended to hamper the
development of the city's left bank, now known as the University or Latin Quarter, although to the west a flood plain
did facilitate development.   On the right bank a semicircle
of heights stretching from the Seine wheeled from east to
west to constitute at first the boundary of the river, but a
change in course created a bordering meander plain which
offered the city a better opportunity for expansion when it
began to push out its foothold on the banks. [17]   This right
bank owed its development principally to the mercantile
quarter near the island city, and it thus acquired the character of the central business quarter which it still maintains.[18]

The natural division of the site of Paris thus corresponds to an organic division of the city: the island city itself, the Ile de la Cité, which is the official and religious
center of Paris; the Latin Quarter on the left bank, which is
the University of Paris; and the mercantile quarter or business district on the right bank, known as the "town. "   This
division accounts for the old expression, "the town, city and
university of Paris. "[19]   The characteristics of each persisted, although inevitably modified and overlaid with the
passage of time.

Notes

1.   David Douglas, "The Paris of Abelard and St. Louis, "
       <u>Cities of Destiny</u>, Arnold Toynbee, editor (New York:
       McGraw-Hill Book Company, 1967), p. 192.

2.   Robert Laffont (ed.), <u>The Illustrated History of Paris
       and the Parisians</u> (Garden City, New York: Double-
       day and Company, 1958), p. 6.

3.   Blake Ehrlich, <u>Paris on the Seine</u> (New York: Athene-
       um, 1962), p. 4.

4. Leopold Genicot, Contours of the Middle Ages (London: Routledge and Kegan Paul, 1967), p. 168.

5. Ibid.

6. Douglas, op. cit., p. 187.

7. Ibid., p. 178.

8. Lewis Mumford, The City in History (New York: Harcourt, Brace and World, Inc., 1961). Responsibility for the application of these concepts is the writer's.

9. Arnold Toynbee (ed.), "Foreword, " Cities of Destiny, op. cit., pp. 104-5.

10. "Paris, " Encyclopaedia Britannica (1964 ed.), XVII, 285.

11. Ibid.

12. Douglas, op. cit., p. 85.

13. "Paris, " op. cit., p. 285.

14. Laffont, op. cit., p. 4.

15. Ibid., p. 148.

16. Joan Evans, Life in Medieval France (revised edition; London: Phaidon Press, 1957), p. 64.

17. "Paris, " op. cit., p. 285.

18. Ibid., p. 288.

19. Ibid.

Chapter 1

PARIS: THE MERCANTILE CITY

Although medieval Paris achieved its pre-eminence as a royal city, an ecclesiastical city, and a university city, no historical sketch, however brief, could fail to recognize the function of the mercantile quarter and its contribution to the development of the city.

With the growth of commerce in the eleventh century a mercantile quarter developed, deriving its origin from the intersection of the course of the river and the land route represented by the two streets of the Rue Saint-Martin and the Rue Saint-Denis. The merchants' thoroughfare was the section of the street called the Juiverie, which ran centrally through the Ile de la Cité, connecting the two bridges. Being the most strategic of mercantile locations, the business energy of the Juiverie soon spilled over the Grand-Pont to the right bank, imparting to it a commercial character which it has never since lost.[1]

The right bank became the commercial and industrial area of the city with individual trades often tending to predominate in certain quarters. In the middle of the twelfth century it was one large marketplace, its narrow streets lined with shops. The Grand-Pont, on which the money-changers had their shops, became the Pont-au-Change in 1142.[2] Les Halles was already situated on the Grève, and meat was sold on the Boucherie. To the east, activity centered about the Knights Templar, who were establishing the Paris temple.[3] Out in the fields beyond the temple stood the fortified royal priory of Saint-Martin-des-Champs, founded ages earlier. Built in 1040 by Henri I on the extension of the Rue Saint-Martin, it gathered within its walls the religious activity of the right bank. The Benedictines of Cluny had made it their center of religious life. Its chapel was the first Gothic building of Paris.[4] Farther off were a cemetery and a leprosarium, and across the marshy plain rose the hill of Montmartre with its abbey on the summit.

In the late twelfth century this mercantile quarter was surrounded by the rampart of Philip Augustus. [5]

    While the commercial development of the city was
notable, it was always secondary in significance, for medieval Paris developed no "heavy" major industries, and if its
crafts were distinguished they were not peculiar to itself.
These merchants, traders, and craftsmen to whom the mercantile quarter owed its growth provisioned the great capital
of Paris, met the needs of the court and the aristocracy
gathered in it, and ministered to the crowds of students who
lived on the left bank. In the thirteenth century, great mercantile houses arose; small traders dealt in meat, fish,
wine; drapers and merchants in cloth formed early connec-
tions with the cloth manufacturers of the Flemish towns;
mercers dealt not only in ordinary apparel but in silks and
furs from the north as well. [6] Later, luxury trades developed and in their turn administered to the arts; for example,
gold and silver ornaments were made and decoration of manuscripts played a large part in Parisian commerce--so large,
it is said, that Dante gave it special mention in his Divine
Comedy. [7] Banking also developed, attracting those interested
in the money market into the city. All of these activities had
their place in the teeming mercantile life of medieval Paris,
but Paris only represented the reproduction on a large scale
of the economic life of any large medieval city.

    The organization of the economic life in thirteenth-
century Paris was typical. This was the age of the craft
guilds. As elsewhere, each craft had its separate organization, fostering the welfare of its members, regulating production and wages, supervising its relations with the outside
world, controlling its membership, insisting upon professional competence by means of its apprenticeship system.
Only after the age of Saint Louis in the late thirteenth century did the system begin to break down with the rise of a
new class of capitalists who obtained an ever-increasing control of industry. Although the municipal life of Paris was
to be stormy in the later Middle Ages, in the earlier thirteenth century an almost perfect social equilibrium existed
between the large body of independent craftsmen organized
into guilds and a smaller body of wealthier merchants. [8] So
long as it lasted, it provided a life of self-respect to the
small traders and at the same time gave the wealthier merchants a political opportunity to impart a sense of communal
self-consciousness to the city they aspired to rule. [9] The
earliest guilds were formed in Paris in the eleventh century,

and the most famous was that of the river traders who plied
up and down the Seine.   It was originally these river traders,
the Company of Water Merchants--the shipbuilders, traders,
warehousemen and shipowners--who won the right of self-
government for the municipality.[10]

Medieval miniatures from the Life of St. Denis capture
vividly the life of the mercantile sector.   These miniatures
show scenes on the Grand-Pont, the city's commercial center.
In one miniature four men drag a barrel loaded on a trolley
across the bridge while a barefooted pilgrim, his shoes hung
around his neck, enters at the right.[11]   A shepherd and his
flock pass a countryman and his pig.   Boats carrying melons
from Meudon, Chaillot or Nogent approach their mooring at
a nearby wharf.   A man with one leg has his eye on a pie;
below, a man stands on the edge of a boat holding his nose,
ready to dive.   A boat laden with casks wants to pass
through, but a toll must be paid; meanwhile, the revenue of-
ficer samples the wine.   In another scene a loaded passenger
carriage enters the covered section of the bridge, and in
another an apothecary cries his salves.   Other scenes from
the same manuscript show a flour mill with its waterwheels
set between the arches of the Grand-Pont.   Although a "mill-
ers' bridge" was built in 1296, the paddle wheels of the
Grand-Pont continued to grind the grain of Beauce.[12]   In yet
another detail three craftsmen work at their metal trades.[13]
These miniatures accentuate the importance of the quays to
the commercial life of the city and indicate the essential function of the river as an inter-urban highway.

In the thirteenth century the trade guilds of Paris had
remodeled the ancient core of the Ile de la Cité to suit their
own needs, constructing the spacious quays on which goods
were loaded and received.   The activities of the mercantile
sector effected a decisive change in the morphology of the
city, stressing a shift in orientation from the concentric design of the earlier cathedral city, which had developed out-
wardly from the Ile de la Cité, to that of a linear merchant
city.   This trend toward linearity was to become more pronounced in the sixteenth century.[14]

A miniature from the Grandes Chroniques de France
shows the Bishop of Paris giving his blessing at the annual
Lendit Fair.   When the Cathedral of Notre Dame acquired a
piece of the True Cross in 1109, it was shown to the people
on the second Wednesday of each June.[15]   Although the Procession of the Relic and the Benediction formed the center

of the occasion, traders were attracted by the large numbers
of pilgrims. Thus the fair of Lendit had its origin in a religious festival. It derived its name from the Latin word
indictum, meaning assembly, which corrupted into l'endit and
then "Lendit." The place chosen for the fair was a large
open space on the road to Saint Denis.[16] This road was a
continuation of the Rue Saint-Denis, which was the main
north-south artery of the growing commercial district on the
right bank.[17]

Les Halles

        The form of a street, or of a square, or of a market
either, was never permanently fixed in medieval cities ex-
cept by artificial controls. Infinitely expanding public space
and ever-encroaching buildings remained in a fluid balance,
affected by the change in the scale and importance of contrasting forces.[18] This was as true of the design of the
city as of its physical structures. Les Halles, the main
produce market of Paris, is the dominant structure of the
mercantile quarter. When it was first established by royal
charter in 1137, the Les Halles market was literally in the
fields, located outside the then existing limits of Paris.
The earlier market on the river bank in the Place de Grève
had become too confined by the encroachment of buildings
and isolated by the gradual crumbling of the old Roman
bridge. With the new commercial center now focused on the
Saint-Jacques la Boucherie quarter at the head of the new
bridge leading to the Rue Saint-Denis, the new market was
transferred to a site which at that time was the periphery of
town. Gradually engulfed by the expanding city during the
twelfth century, the market of Les Halles was eventually incorporated within Philip Augustus' wall around 1200. Many
monarchs rebuilt and expanded the markets. The ultimate
shape of Les Halles is the product of the funnels formed at
the heads of the streets entering the marketplace from all
directions.[19]

        Procurement, storage, distribution: these were the
functions of the marketplace of Les Halles, itself largely a
product of the securities and regularities of urban life. Les
Halles translated into physical form the primary function of
Paris, the mercantile city: the production and exchange of
goods and services. The city of Paris with its efficient
means of mass transport by water and by land routes, and
through the agency of its marketplace, made it possible to
equalize surpluses and to have access to distant specialties.

With the wider distribution of the goods in the marketplace came the widening of the communication system that had grown up along with it.[20]

Bourgeoisie

The new class in society, composed of craftsmen, artisans, merchants and traders whose prosperity derived from the building and provisioning of the capital and the trade and the taxes which the junction of land routes, rivers, and quays attracted, was the bourgeoisie. From the early decades of the twelfth century, their activity was concentrated on the right bank.

Although the bourgeoisie of Paris had its counterpart in most of the great cities, the special interest attaching to the Parisian bourgeoisie in the thirteenth century, vigorously active as it was in providing for an urban population, derived not so much from its share in an economic activity that was common to Western Europe at this time, but rather from its close relationship with the monarchy. From the first, this connection between the monarchy and the bourgeoisie was apparent, and they had their own special part to play in the government of France.[21] Philip Augustus not only added to the defense of the city with his wall begun in 1180, but he made the citizens of Paris francs bourgeois, with a provost and a council of six burghers.[22] When the king was about to depart on a crusade in 1190, he entrusted the royal treasure and the royal seal to these six burghers. In every town representatives of the bourgeoisie stood side by side with the royal officials. The royal system of government with its well-paid officials was much closer to the bourgeois world than to the feudal one which it was to supersede.[23] Men flocked to the city; numbers and prosperity increased.[24] Crafts, trades, and commerce flourished and continued to flourish. Population was doubling with each generation, and people were building with feverish haste to keep pace with the expansion.[25] Paris had become the royal capital, and as the power of the Capets grew, so too did the importance of the citizens of their capital. Nevertheless, the bourgeoisie did not achieve the degree of preeminence enjoyed by the other prime institutions of medieval Paris: the Monarchy, the Church, and the University.[26]

12   Medieval Paris

Notes

1. "Paris," Encyclopaedia Britannica (1964 ed.), XVII, 286.

2. Ibid.

3. Allan Temko, Notre-Dame of Paris (Time Reading Program special edition; New York: Time Incorporated, 1955), p. 71.

4. Laffont, op. cit., p. 33.

5. "Paris," op. cit., p. 286.

6. Douglas, op. cit., p. 192.

7. Ibid.

8. Ibid., p. 193.

9. Ibid.

10. Ehrlich, op. cit., p. 4.

11. Douglas, op. cit., pp. 184-85, citing the Life of St. Denis, 1317 (MS in the Bibliothèque Nationale, Paris).

12. Laffont, op. cit., p. 46.

13. Douglas, op. cit., pp. 184-85, citing the Life of St. Denis.

14. Sibyl Moholy-Nagy, Matrix of Man (New York: Frederick A. Praeger, 1968), p. 213, Figure 215.

15. Douglas, op. cit., p. 185, citing the Grandes Chroniques de France, fourteenth century (MS in the Musée Goya, Castres).

16. Donald King, "Industry, Merchants and Money," The Flowering of the Middle Ages, Joan Evans, editor (New York: McGraw-Hill Book Company, 1966), p. 262.

17. Howard Saalman, Medieval Cities (in Planning and

Cities Series, ed. George R. Collins. New York:
George Braziller, 1968), p. 34.

18. Ibid., pp. 34-35.

19. Ibid.

20. Mumford, op. cit., p. 71.

21. Douglas, op. cit., p. 192.

22. Evans, op. cit., p. 64.

23. Fritz Rörig, The Medieval Town (Berkeley, California:
University of California Press, 1967), p. 60.

24. Evans, op. cit., p. 64.

25. Temko, op. cit., p. 66.

26. Douglas, op. cit., p. 178.

Chapter 2

PARIS: THE ROYAL CITY

Medieval Paris did achieve its pre-eminence in
Europe as a royal city. On the island in the Seine is where
Paris, the royal city, began. The history of Paris flows
past the shores of the Seine, and the stones of Paris speak
of the city caught in its long history. The present blends
with the past. The stones of an old façade conceal the
shadow of a beautiful, plotting woman; the stones of an ancient square are stained with traces of riots and massacres;
the stones of the Louvre rumble with seven centuries of history; the stones of Notre Dame Cathedral are filled with a
great vaulted silence. The history of Paris reflects the
history of France and, to a large extent, the history of
Western Europe. Over the centuries, the city of Paris
brought together and shaped into a visible unity, fortress,
shrine, school; but the character of the city altered from
age to age as one force then another--now Church, now
Monarchy, now University or Bourgeoisie--dominated and influenced the others.

In Roman days the Ile de la Cité was known as "Lutetia. " In 53 B.C., Caesar's centurions took the island city
of Lutetia from an unimportant tribe of the lower Seine
called the Parisii. Caesar describes his "dear Lutetia" as
being surrounded on all sides by the river and connected to
each bank by wooden bridges. In his Commentaries, Caesar
tells of the burning of Lutetia during the Gallic Wars.[1]

Under Roman rule during the first century A.D., the
character of Lutetia changed. As a Roman town, it spread
beyond its island to the left bank; the low-lying, uninviting
ground of the right bank discouraged expansion. A new Roman settlement grew up on the northern slopes of the left
bank's Mons Lucotitius, characterized by the straight roads
and the public buildings typical of all Roman towns--the
forum, the public baths, the theatre, the amphitheatre, the
aqueduct. Lutetia spread up the hillside and was unfortified.

14

Its cemetery lay by the side of the Roman road, later known
as the Rue Saint-Jacques. The Roman city of Lutetia was
not important; administratively, it was subject to Sens. [2]

During the barbarian invasions from the third century
onward, Lutetia suffered severely and its inhabitants de-
serted the left bank and the new districts on the right and
gathered again within the limits of the original island, hem-
ming it in with a wall seven and half feet thick at a distance
of about thirty yards from the river. Confined within this
narrow space, the city possessed few public buildings, probably a temple in the east and a palatium, or palace of the
governor, in the west. It remained connected with the two
banks by the bridges. At this same period the name "Lutetia" was altered: a milestone dated 307 on the way to Rheims
records the name of "Paris" for the first time. [3]

With the breakdown of Roman administration, the
settlement of Paris slowly declined. Continuity was, here
as elsewhere, maintained through the permanence of the ecclesiastical organization which inherited much of the Roman
political system. Roman buildings crumbled; vegetation
spread over the baths and administrative buildings; and no
secular ruler came to revive the splendor of the Roman
past. [4]

When the Franks made themselves masters of Paris
in the fifth century, they did not destroy the Roman civilization; they were influenced by its more advanced culture.
With their conversion to Christianity under Clovis, they came
doubly under the influence of Rome. Although Clovis chose
to establish his capital at Paris in order to bring the seat
of authority closer to the newly conquered territories, and
although several of his Merovingian successors had made
Paris their capital--among them Clotaire in 558, Chilperic
in 561, Caribert in 567--the kings usually resided elsewhere.[5]
Paris was just a castle town. Not yet was it a big market
town nor a commercial center nor a cultural center. The
city was above all at this time a center of religious life,
hallowed by the memory of Sainte-Geneviève, who had
watched over it at the time of the Hunnish invasions. [6]

During the Carolingian period Paris lost most of what
importance it had gained as a capital. Charlemagne looked
rather to Rome and to Aachen, while his successors reigned
from Laon. The Holy Roman Empire was centered to the
east, and the royal dynasts moved from Metz to Aachen.

To counterbalance the influence of the bishops, the kings established the counts as his representatives, and these counts
grew more and more independent.[7]

Paris waited long before it became the capital city.
Something more than a strategic geographical location was
required. An existing city, says Toynbee, may be made into a capital city by virtue of its having acquired prestige
through playing an heroic part at some crisis in a people's
history.[8] It was in the work of preserving Western civilization in its darkest hour that Paris emerged into the European
consciousness as a capital city in the true sense. The historical role of Paris began with the successful defense of
the counts of Paris between 885 and 887 against the wave of
Norse expansion, which all but submerged Western Christendom under pagan domination.[9] The Norman invasions made
havoc of the city. This historical crisis was one of the
turning points in the history of Europe. Neither the city nor
its secular rulers ever lost the prestige which they then won.
Partly because of this, Paris was able in 987 to supplant
Laon as the capital of France.[10]

In the early tenth century, while the Robertian counts
were superseding the Carolingian kings, the land around the
city was brought under cultivation. There were patches of
woods and some swamps, but few hamlets. Paris at this
time may be regarded as the juxtaposition of the centers of
a number of great domains, principally ecclesiastical domains, and was in fact a sort of feudal mosaic.[11] When a
successor of the early counts named Hugh Capet established
a new dynasty in France in 987, this dynasty succeeded to
a thoroughly feudalized domain, and the Capetian kings had
to defend it against ambitious vassals who held great fiefs
outside it.[12] After the accession of the Capetians, the feudal suzerain was at the same time the king of the country.
This Capetian dynasty was centered in Paris, and Paris became a capital city. The more the monarchy increased in
power and extended its influence over France, the more
Paris grew in importance.[13] From these beginnings medieval Paris, the royal city, arose.

The fifteen kings who ruled France from 987 to 1328
are called collectively "the Capetians of the direct line" because from Hugh Capet, who succeeded the last of the Caro-
lingians, to the last of the Capetian dynasty, Louis X, son
succeeded father without interruption. With the death of
Louis X, the crown passed to the Valois line. Following a

general discussion of the achievements of the Capetian dynasty, the focus rests upon the two most outstanding rulers, Philip II Augustus and Louis IX, and their contributions to the development of the city of Paris.[14]

The achievements of the Capetians were great. Directing their energies mainly into practical politics, these Capetian rulers worked with steady perseverance to establish, organize, and increase the power of the monarchy.[15] At the end of the tenth century, the Capetian kingdom was only a diminutive domain called the Ile de France, an old district forming a kind of island extending from Paris to Orleans, with Paris as its capital. The name referred to the royal lands under the direct control of the king, while the rest of what is now France was still under the dominion of feudal lords. This domain was much smaller and weaker than that of many a great vassal.[16] By 1328, which marked the end of the Capetian line, the kingdom of France was the most powerful in Western Europe, extending over the greater part of France and excluding only the four large fiefs of Flanders, Brittany, Burgundy, and Aquitane.[17]

Under the Capetian kings the character of Paris again underwent change. The capital city of the new monarchy grew slowly from the late tenth to the early twelfth century. When Hugh Capet chose the island city of Paris for his capital, the ancient town had shrunk to the Ile de la Cité itself, with a few buildings on either bank.[18] At the beginning of the eleventh century, the hamlets which had grown around each of the monasteries still remained distinct from the central Paris of the Cité. This central settlement was marked with the desolation of ancient decay. From the twelfth century onward, with the reign of Philip Augustus, the city grew rapidly.[19]

The expansion of the royal domain strengthened the Capetians economically and militarily. Economically, the influence of the Capetians was important but indirect. By enforcing order within the kingdom, by giving it strong institutions, and by protecting the merchants, the Capetians contributed to the accumulation of wealth in France. The growth of the royal domain and of the king's power, together with the progress of ideas, led to a reorganization of the government. With the new institutions which came into being as the kings gradually modified the system, the authority of the king could be exercised more effectively.[20] Militarily, a relentless war against the Albigenses was fought under papal

orders by the kings of France and the nobles of the north
against the south, ending in the humiliation of the princes of
the south, in the destruction of the famous Provençal culture,
and in the extermination of the Albigensian heresy. The last
major military expedition, which was led by Louis VIII, resulted in the annexation of the county of Toulouse. [21]

Much of the success of the Capetians was due to the
active support of the clergy, who wanted to see peace and
order prevail in the kingdom; to the religious character
which the ceremony of the king's coronation gave to the
monarchy; and to the cooperation of the bourgeoisie. [22] The
French monarchy generally maintained good relations with
the papacy and most often helped the popes. They also
aided in the foundation of monasteries by giving donations
and protection. The Capetians participated in the Crusades
more actively than any other dynasty then reigning in Europe. The prestige of the dynasty, consecrated as it was by
its link with the papacy, enabled the kings to prevail against
their rivals. [23]

While the Capetians did not interfere directly in the
development of thought in France from the end of the tenth
century to the beginning of the fourteenth, they nevertheless
had a share in that development. The order that prevailed
under them, the protection that they granted to the learned,
and the care that Philip Augustus and his successors took
to enhance the prestige of Paris contributed indirectly to intellectual development. They were friends of the university
and fostered its development, but secular thought and literature in the vernacular also developed considerably. [24] By
providing a broad kingdom made up of richly varied but
peaceful provinces, the center of which was the great city
of Paris, the Capetians provided an ideal setting for a
flourishing culture.

Under Philip II Augustus, who succeeded in 1180,
France emerged as a nation. After declaring King John of
England to have forfeited all the fiefs he held of the French
crown, Philip went on to conquer Normandy and other English possessions with the exception of Aquitane. He further
extended his realm through marriage or conquest or confis-
cation from Cherbourg to the Pyrenees. [25]

The close connection between the Capetians and their
capital city reached a climax with Philip II Augustus. He
was a friend of the bourgeoisie and surrounded himself with

clerks and law specialists of more or less humble origin who gave him counsel and acted as his agents.[26] He provided strong institutions, two of which were the bailiff in the north and the steward in the south, to administer local territories, to collect taxes for the Crown, and to try cases. Each man was assigned a district, and if he proved to be an able civil servant he was given another assignment; if not, he was dismissed.[27]

Philip Augustus favored the great merchants, granting them trade privileges and monopolies, and he was the ally and protector of the communes. Before his reign, the communes were resisted and often crushed; after his reign, they were exploited, oppressed, and finally destroyed. Although he suppressed some communes in the newly conquered fiefs such as Normandy, he erected new communes in his own private domain, which was quite contrary to the custom of other kings.[28]

The feudal system was the source of the tyranny of the lords over the bourgeoisie, as well as of the revolt of the same lords against the king. When kings were strong, therefore, the nobles were kept under control and the people prospered. Thus a close relationship developed between the king and the bourgeoisie, who naturally fostered the communes against the nobles. Philip Augustus seems to have regarded the communes as a kind of defense against the nobles, while the rents which they furnished increased his financial resources.[29] Philip Augustus, incidentally, amassed a sizeable treasury, but he reinvested much of it in the development of the city.[30]

From the twelfth century onward the royal power increased, and the king held himself to be sovereign over the whole feudal system.[31] With this new status, the royal capital of Philip Augustus had a new social as well as a political role to play. Philip Augustus added to the amenities of the city, and society became more sophisticated and more urbane. "To be a free burgess," wrote Renart le Contrefait, "is to be in the best estate of all; they live in a noble manner, wearing lordly garments, having falcons and sparrowhawks, fine palfreys and fine chargers."[32] In this capital, which was the home of royalty and aristocracy, provincial habits, customs, and dialects were blended and then refined in the image of the royal court, and this then became the national image--"national, " that is, by imitative fashion rather than by origin. Paris became the royal capital, which conferred upon the monarchy a unique luster.

Louis IX, grandson of Philip II Augustus, continued the centralization effected by Philip Augustus. His over-throw of the independent counts of Toulouse during the re-ligious wars against the Albigenses enlarged the kingdom of France so that it gained a seaboard on the Mediterranean, on the Atlantic, and on the English Channel. Louis IX left local administration in the hands of the bailiffs and the stew-ards, but he added the institution of the "inquisitor," a good-will representative of the royal court, whose purpose it was to hear complaints of all subjects whatever their rank. The people could report their grievances directly to the inquisitor, over the head of the bailiff or steward, and the king would then right the wrong. The reputation of Louis as a fair judge brought appeals from all parts of Christendom. [33]

King Louis IX was one of the greatest of the Capetians. While Philip Augustus pursued his policy of building a strong monarchy with a persistence which excluded scruple, his grandson, who held a high conception of the office, rights and duties of a king, sought not only to live but to rule ac-cording to the precepts of religion. King Louis IX was powerful enough to implement his theories, and by the end of his reign no part of the kingdom was without some tie to the government. [34]

King Louis was renowned for his sanctity, but his piety did not lead him into subservience to the Church. Al-though he spent hours at prayer and had people fed at public expense, sometimes waiting on them himself, yet he brought the clergy under civil jurisdiction. He lived his faith, and he expressed this faith in action. He founded hospitals, asylums, homes for the blind, homes for reformed prosti-tutes. [35]

The achievements of King Louis IX and his reputation for sanctity brought immense prestige to the Capetian mon-archy. Respect for the power of royal government and per-sonal regard for the king bred loyalty to the monarchy as an institution. [36] His nobility lent an incomparable luster to French royalty. "The throne of France," wrote Jean de Joinville in his Histoire de Saint Louis, "was resplendent in the eyes of all others, like the sun which sends forth its rays."[37] In later times his reign was regarded as a period of great prosperity and happiness, and he was canonized by Pope Boniface VIII in August of 1297. [38]

The life and the labors which Philip Augustus and Louis IX and other Capetian rulers undertook are reflected in the physical structures which each had erected. In these physical structures, past events, decisions made long ago, values formulated and achieved, remain alive. The translation of personal choices into physical structures is a function of the city.[39]

Every advance in Capetian power was reflected in the morphology of the city. The close relationship between the Capetians and their capital city reached its height in the century from the rule of Philip II Augustus beginning in 1180 to the death of Louis IX in 1270. Symptomatic of this connection between monarchy and their city is the old tale relating the story of Philip Augustus sitting in the palace that had been built on Roman foundations, gazing at the muddy waters of the river and brooding over the city which lay around him.[40] Under the Capetians, this unbroken connection culminated in the Golden Age of Paris.

Philip Augustus was the real builder of Paris. During the period when king and knights left for the Crusades and Paris had to protect itself, Philip Augustus surrounded his city with a rampart. The city of Paris became a fortress. Begun some time after 1180, the rampart was extended to the right bank in 1190 and to the left bank in 1209.[41] The city was encircled by this unbroken wall thirty feet high and between seven and ten feet thick, defended by thirty-three towers on the right bank and thirty-four on the left. It had twelve gates. A solid piece of work, time alone could break it down. The wall survives today only in fragments.[42] A section of the rampart stretching along the Seine in front of the imposing mass of the Louvre is represented as it was in the late fourteenth century, with its balconies and towers and posterns, in the illumination of "October" painted by the Limbourg brothers for The Très Riches Heures of Jean, Duke of Berry. Tiny figures stroll on the quay from which steps lead to the river, giving access to the boats.[43] The rampart bore witness to the existence of the city standing astride the Seine. Within these walls, Paris became a civic unit.

Within those city walls Philip Augustus directed his efforts toward improvement, and his reign was marked by something of a transformation of the city. He engineered the first water supply of Paris. As the city expanded over the Grand-Pont to the right bank, it experienced a shortage

of water. Philip made a catchment of the springs from the
heights of Belleville. The first public fountains appeared in
Les Halles and in the Charnier des Innocents nearby. The
Fontaine Maubuée, decorated with the arms of Paris and
situated at the corner of the Rue Saint-Martin, was to provide the citizens of Paris with water for seven centuries. [44]
Philip Augustus paved the streets of the city with stone. [45]
Cobblestones can be seen in a detail from one of the illuminations in the fourteenth-century manuscript of the Life of St.
Denis, referred to above. Bridges, quays, barges; man-
drawn trolleys and horse-drawn carriages; cobblestoned streets
and covered bridges; flour mill and metal-working establishment, all of which are illustrated in the miniatures, bear
witness to the enterprise and efficiency of this Capetian ruler,
to the decisions he made and to the values he formulated
and achieved.

Louvre

        Prominent in the morphology of medieval Paris was
the Louvre, most impressive of the city's monuments. The
original Louvre was built by Philip Augustus, shortly after
1200, as a royal residence. This feudal bastion was planned
to defend the entrance to the city wall at the spot where
three hundred and fifty years earlier the Normans had
camped in their last great siege of Paris. The chateau was
square and the moated central tower, the dungeon, was a
fortress within a fortress. A great central stronghold, one
hundred and forty-four feet in circumference, ninety-six feet
in height, with walls thirteen feet thick, this dungeon was
immensely strong. From this stronghold, where the king's
military strength was centered, the garrison had a clear
view westward across fields and forest toward the Anglo-
Norman enemy, and eastward across Paris above Les Halles
and the Boucherie to the fortified temple. It served as a
strong-room for the royal archives and as a royal prison as
much as for a tower of defense; here too the royal treasury
was housed. [46] One of its deepest dungeons survives, its
stunted pillars ornamented with carved heads. [47]

        Philip Augustus called this tower of defense "our
tower of the Louvre." Scholars do not seem to agree on the
origin of the name, but it is believed the name may perhaps
derive from the Viking word "leovar, " meaning "camp. "[48]
This first Louvre was torn down in the sixteenth century
when the present palace was begun. The splendor of the

castle when it was newly built and in active use can still be
seen in contemporary paintings. The original Louvre is illustrated in the miniature representing "October, " referred
to above, from the manuscript The Très Riches Heures. In
this miniature, the dungeon hides the northwest tower where
Charles V kept the precious manuscripts of his library, but
the other three corners are visible, as is the eastern façade
protected by twin towers. Every detail is so precisely
drawn that it was possible for Viollet-le-Duc to reconstruct
a model of it several centuries after its destruction. [49] At
least seventeen monarchs participated in the building of this
monument which took about seven hundred years to complete. [50]

The dominance of the mass and profile of the Louvre
in the morphology of medieval Paris proclaims its identity
as a royal city. The structure of the Louvre translated into
physical form the magnification of secular power and symbolized the royal prerogative.

As a capital city, the function of Paris expanded, and
it became the seat of law and justice, of reason and equity.
By putting power in some measure at the service of justice,
the city brought order more swiftly into its internal affairs.
Power, concentrated in the person of the king toward whom
the life of the whole city was focused, brightened into social
justice under the reign of Louis the Saint. Although power
was the mainstay of Paris as the capital city of the Capets,
it became increasingly shaped and directed by new institutions of law and order, by new social customs and urbanity.
With the expanded function of the capital city came the rise
of an official bureaucracy with its clerks and permanent officials and new bureaucratic functions--the establishment of
archives, deeds, tax records, the promulgation of rules and
regulations. A separate ruling class of king and royal court,
by use of deliberate withdrawal and detachment to break into
the cycle of production, exchange, and consumption of goods,
gained control of the creative processes. Although much of
the surplus produced in urban society was spent on extrava-
gent consumption and even more extravagant acts of military
destruction, much of it went into uncommitted leisure time
which, when released from the daily routine, was devoted to
the contemplation of nature and discipline of the human mind.
Activities reserved for festive occasions, such as expressions
of drama, poetry, music, and dance, became a part of the
daily life of the city. Through the performance of creative
acts in art and thought and in personal relationships, the
capital city came to be identified as something more than a

fortress city, more than a functional organization of barracks,
courts, dungeons, and royal control. Men who were originally attracted to the city by the security and stability it offered remained there to live a purposeful life.

The character of Paris, the royal city, was reflected
in the city's design. Segregated social roles created equivalent precincts within the city, and the Ile de la Cité became
the seat of the royal court. Walls, ramparts, barracks,
dungeons, the palace of the Louvre towering grimly above
the city, always threatening to resume its original preroga-
tives: these were the architectural symbols that made visible the function of the city of Paris as a center of control.
The function of Paris, the royal city, supplemented its functions as a mercantile city and as an ecclesiastical city.

The figure of the Capetian king who stands astride
two worlds--the world of Paris, the royal city, and the
world of Paris, the ecclesiastical city--is that of Louis IX,
called Saint Louis. During his reign, the function of the
royal city and that of the ecclesiastical city merged into one.

Sainte-Chapelle

Sainte-Chapelle in Paris is an example of a royal
private chapel. It stands as a testimonial to the values formulated and achieved by Louis IX, the Saint. Where Philip
Augustus had reluctantly led an expedition to the Holy Land
during the Third Crusade (1190-92), Louis IX conceived, organized, and commanded the Seventh (1248-54) and also the
Eighth Crusade, but met his death at the beginning of the
latter.[51] Sainte-Chapelle is the shrine which Saint Louis
was inspired to create as a shelter for the Crown of Thorns
and other holy relics of the Passion: two pieces of the
True Cross, a fragment of the spear, a bit of the vinegar
sponge, shreds of clothing, the reed which the Romans had
thrust upon Jesus as a scepter, together with a nail from
the True Cross which had been obtained earlier during the
First Crusade. The crusader king did not win these relics
at lance point from the Saracens, but purchased them from
John of Brienne, emperor of Constantinople.[52]

Completed in 1249, Sainte-Chapelle initiated an architectural form which was to become common to royal chapels:
it consisted of two levels, a lower chapel which supported
an upper chapel level with the state apartments.[53] The

Sainte-Chapelle is an exquisite piece of ecclesiastical architecture, often quoted as a typical Gothic structure, with the
space between the buttresses occupied by a profusion of
stained glass windows fifteen feet wide and fifty feet high
which completely dissolve the walls. [54] Located near Notre
Dame Cathedral and now within the precincts of the Palais
de Justice, the frothy spires which crest the chapel soar into the sky, [55] typifying the religious fervor of the Paris of
Saint Louis. The master glassmakers illustrated one thousand one hundred and thirty-four scenes in the stained glass
windows of Sainte-Chapelle, in which the Old Testament, the
Gospels, and the Apocalypse combine in a mass of color.
The only contemporary sequence is the solemn voyage of the
Crown of Thorns, each stage of which is illustrated in minute detail. [56] The royal party took eight days to carry the
reliquary, barefooted and clad in simple tunics, from Sens
to Paris where, accompanied by a brilliant procession which
followed them through the city, it was placed at last in a
chapel of Notre Dame to await completion of the shrine. [57]
One scene shows Saint Louis and his brothers bearing the
triple casket of wood, silver, and gold containing this most
moving of the relics, the Crown of Thorns.

Sainte-Chapelle also served as a private room for the
religious contemplation of Saint Louis. First king of France
to realize the value and importance of books, Saint Louis set
aside, in the room next to the treasury of relics, a library
for study in his leisure time, and he opened it to others who
wished to work there. Here were placed the works of Augustine, Jerome, Gregory, and others. [58] Here too was
placed an illuminated manuscript, glowing with gold and lapis
lazuli, [59] inspiring and inspired, its very presence in this
shrine a testimonial to the medieval attitude of awe and reverence toward the book, which at this time was regarded as
a sacred object.

Sainte-Chapelle is a rarity, a translation into physical
form of the values of a rare man become saint; a lofty idea
whose expression matches the conception.

Notes

1.   "Paris, " op. cit., p. 285.

2.   Ibid. , pp. 285-86.

3. Ibid., p. 286.

4. Douglas, op. cit., p. 188.

5. "Paris," op. cit., p. 286.

6. Ibid.

7. Ibid.

8. Arnold Toynbee, Cities on the Move (New York: Ox-
    ford University Press, 1970), p. 83.

9. Douglas, op. cit., p. 188.

10. Toynbee, Cities on the Move, op. cit., p. 83.

11. "Paris," op. cit., p. 286.

12. "France," Encyclopaedia Britannica (1964 ed.), IX,
    702-3.

13. "Paris," op. cit., p. 286.

14. The Capetian succession is presented for convenience
    of reference: Hugh Capet (987-996), Robert II the
    Pious (996-1031), Henry I (1031-1060), Philip I
    (1060-1108), Louis VI (1108-1137), Louis VII (1137-
    1180), Philip II Augustus (1180-1223), Louis VIII
    (1223-1226), Louis IX (Saint Louis; 1226-1270),
    Philip III the Bold (1270-1285), Philip IV the Fair
    (1285-1314), and Louis X le Hutin or the Stubborn
    (1314-1316). Since Louis X's posthumous son, offi-
    cially reckoned as John I (1316), died a few days
    after his birth, the crown then went successively
    to Louis X's two brothers, Philip V the Tall (1316-
    1322), and Charles IV the Fair (1322-1328).
    "France," op. cit., pp. 702-3.

15. Ibid., p. 703.

16. Ibid.

17. Ibid.

18. Ibid.

19. Douglas, op. cit., p. 188.

20. "France," op. cit., p. 705.

21. Ibid., p. 704.

22. Ibid.

23. Ibid., p. 702.

24. Ibid., p. 705.

25. Anne Fremantle and others, Age of Faith (Great Ages of Man Series. New York: Time Incorporated, 1965), p. 146.

26. "Philip II, " Encyclopaedia Britannica (1964 ed.), XVII, 721.

27. Fremantle and others, op. cit., pp. 146-47.

28. "Philip II, " op. cit., p. 721.

29. Ibid.

30. Fremantle and others, op. cit., p. 146.

31. "Philip II, " op. cit., p. 721.

32. Evans, op. cit., p. 64.

33. "Louis IX, " Encyclopaedia Britannica (1964 ed.), XIV, 416.

34. Ibid.

35. Fremantle and others, op. cit., p. 146.

36. Ibid.

37. Rene Huyghe, "Art Forms and Society, " Larousse Encyclopedia of Byzantine and Medieval Art (New York: Prometheus Press, 1963), p. 344, citing Jean de Joinville, Histoire de Saint Louis.

38. "Louis IX, " op. cit., p. 416.

39. Based upon a concept presented by Mumford, op. cit.,
    p. 113. Responsibility for the application of the
    concept is the writer's.

40. Douglas, op. cit., p. 183.

41. "Paris, " op. cit., p. 288.

42. Laffont, op. cit., p. 30.

43. The Très Riches Heures of Jean, Duke of Berry (Re-
    produced from the illuminated manuscript in the
    Musée Condé, Chantilly, France; New York: George
    Braziller, 1969), Figure 11.

44. Laffont, op. cit., p. 32.

45. Douglas, op. cit., p. 184.

46. Ehrlich, op. cit., p. 254.

47. Laffont, op. cit., p. 31.

48. Ibid.

49. Christopher Hohler, "Court Life in Peace and War, "
    The Flowering of the Middle Ages, op. cit., p. 177.

50. Ehrlich, op. cit., p. 253.

51. "France, " op. cit., p. 704.

52. Ehrlich, op. cit., p. 178.

53. Hohler, op. cit., p. 151.

54. Paul Frankl, "Gothic Architecture, " Encyclopaedia Bri-
    tannica (1964 ed.), X, 602.

55. Banister Fletcher, A History of Architecture on the
    Comparative Method (sixteenth edition; New York:
    Charles Scribner's Sons, 1958), p. 386.

56. Laffont, op. cit., pp. 37-39.

57. Temko, op. cit., p. 228.

58. James Westfall Thompson, The Medieval Library (New
     York: Hafner Publishing Company, 1967), p. 258.

59. Ehrlich, op. cit., p. 180.

Chapter 3

PARIS: THE ECCLESIASTICAL CITY

By the middle of the thirteenth century, Paris, the royal capital and fortress city of Philip Augustus, had become, due to the religious influence which pulsated through the royal city of Saint Louis, an ecclesiastical capital whose importance was reflected in the number and character of its churches. The dominance of this religious influence transformed the character of Paris from that of a fortress city into a city of shrines.

Christianity reached Paris in the middle of the third century. Although a tenth-century sacramentary refers to Saint Denis as having been the first bishop of the city, about 250, it was probably during the episcopate of Saint Marcel, the ninth bishop of Paris (c360-436), that Christianity gained a foothold on the island and that an humble wooden church was built there.[1] Nevertheless, it was Saint Denis, his successors and their followers who preserved, albeit with difficulty, the Parisian identity. After Christianity was made the official religion of the Roman Empire in 380, the structure of the church became more elaborate. In the following centuries, the Roman Empire and the tribes that had overwhelmed it together became Christendom.[2]

During the Merovingian period, Paris, hallowed by the memory of Sainte-Geneviève, became a center of religious life. From the fifth to the eighth century the chief persons in the history of Paris were the saints, for whom Parisian churches were named. Chapels and churches thus sprang up, and houses clustered about them amid the vineyards of the left bank and the reeds of the right; for example, the basilica dedicated to the apostles Peter and Paul, and the basilica dedicated to Saint Vincent in which the bishop Germanus was buried. A village developed around the church where Saint Marcel was buried. On the right bank stood the churches of Saints-Gervais-et-Protais and Saint Laurent, and on the low-lying ground to the north, the Basilica of

30

Saint Martin.[3] The old city, however, remained walled-in
on the island. Its Basilica of Notre Dame almost encircled
the fourth-century church of Saint Etienne in the eastern
quarter, just in front of the present site of Notre Dame Cathedral, which was erected as a replacement for both.[4] A
maze of bystreets wound through the city on either side of
the main street joining the two bridges, and suburbs connected this center to the blocks of houses surrounding the
churches.[5]

The Church had thus preserved the continuous life of
Paris through the early Middle Ages, and the kings of the
Capetian house gave it new life. When Hugh Capet chose
Paris for his capital in the tenth century, all but the church
showed signs of decay. The great monasteries, which had
withstood the centuries of decline, faced each other across
the river, Saint-Germain-des-Près, formerly the basilica
dedicated to Saint Vincent, on one side, and Saint-Germain
L'Auxerrois on the other.[6] The abbey of Saint Victor,
founded during the reign of Louis VI, formed a nucleus of
rural population. Sainte-Geneviève stood on the southern
hill and Saint Marcel near what is now the boulevard of that
name, and toward the north, Saint Merry, near the present
Halles.[7] On the left bank, Mons Lucotitius had become the
"Mount" of Sainte-Geneviève.[8] The road through Paris was
dotted all along its length with pious foundations.[9]

In the eleventh century a parish was formed in Paris
near the priory of Saint-Martin-des-Champs. About 1080 the
priory church was also the parish church, but early in the
twelfth century the functions of the parish church were transferred to the neighboring chapel of Saint-Nicolas-des-Champs.
The Church of the Innocents, built about 1150, and the abbey
of Saint Magloire, founded about the same time, bear witness to the increasing population in the neighborhood of Louis
VI's new market.[10] Parish market and parish church ad-
joined each other as the mercantile, legal, and religious
center of the parish unit within the urban structure.[11]

In the late twelfth century, Paris became not only a
city of castles and churches, but a city of miracles. The
miracle concerned the Seine. When the Seine rebels, it is
savage. Ugly, discolored, swollen, it rages against banks
and batters bridges. In the year 1176, during the reign of
the fourth Capet king, whose religiosity had developed marked-
ly after the First Crusade,[12] what was fast becoming the
worst deluge in the history of Paris was halted just before

it flooded the city. The Seine had washed out the two
bridges, crumbled the banks, and carried away houses and
livestock. Louis VII, father of Philip Augustus, with his
court, and the Bishop of Paris, with priests and monks of
the diocese, made their way to the edge of the flood waters.
Here the Bishop, holding aloft the nail from the True Cross,
prayed, "In this sign of the Holy Passion, may the waters
return to their bed and this miserable people be protected!"
The crest fell; the waters ebbed; Paris survived. 13

        The religious zeal of the age when Christianity was
united against the Saracens was manifested in France by the
participation of ruler and ruled in the Crusades. At this
time the clergy had reached the summit of its power, due
largely to its championship of justice and support of the
royal cause. The age was characterized by a religious fervor which found expression in the veneration of saints and
in the cult of relics and Mariolatry. This religiosity was
reflected in the beautiful architecture and decoration of
churches. Urban populations set about building cathedrals
with a rapidity which transformed the face of France, covering it with "a white robe of churches."14 In Paris the
three-century old Basilica of Notre Dame which had replaced
the one destroyed by the Normans was being torn down to
make way for a larger cathedral to accommodate the expanding population. 15 Its wooden ceilings, rude sculpture
and masonry could not compare with the miracles of glass
and stone being constructed in other cities. Redolent with
antiquity, it appeared unworthy to serve as the shrine of
the Virgin of Paris. Pope Alexander III inaugurated a vast
foundation for the new Cathedral of Notre Dame in 1163. 16

        Within his capital city, King Philip II Augustus was
promoting the destiny of Paris. Within the walls which he
erected, churches were being built; sometimes they were
built anew, and sometimes adapted from older Romanesque
churches. While massive Romanesque arches could still be
seen in the abbeys, it was the Gothic impulse which was now
giving expression to the inspiration of the age. On the right
bank, Saint Honoré and Saint Eustache were built in 1223;
on the left bank, the churches of Saint Sulpice, 1211; Saint-
André-des-Arts, c1215; Saint-Etienne-du-Mont, which contained Sainte-Geneviève's sarcophagus, 1222; and Saint-Nico-
las-du-Chardonnet, 1243. 17 Elsewhere, too, churches were
rising, and rural settlements gathered around these churches
and abbeys.

In 1217, Dominique de Guzman sent seven of his followers to Paris where they founded the convent of the Dominicans, later called the convent of the Jacobins, in the
Rue Saint-Jacques. Saint Dominic's successor as head of
the preaching friars, Jourdain of Saxony, was a pupil there,
as were Saint Albert the Great and Saint Thomas Aquinas.[18]
During the reign of Saint Louis, the number of monasteries
increased. After introducing in 1230 the Carmelites, mendicant friars, he installed on the left bank the Franciscans,
or grey friars. In 1254 Saint Louis founded, upon the ad-
vice of his sister, an abbey at Longchamps, while near the
Louvre he also founded a hospice for three hundred blind
persons. For many years his most famous foundation was
the Carthusian monastery of Vauvert, on the site of which
the Luxembourg gardens now stand. This area in the time
of Saint Louis was wooded country outside the city walls,
where Druidic or Gallo-Roman ruins had harbored evil
forces, in particular the devil Vauvert, stories about whom
had lived long in the folk memory. A great collection of
buildings arose there, dominated by the chapel built in 1326,
but nothing of this now remains.[19]

The great cathedral-building epoch corresponded with
the consolidation of the French kingdom and the rise of
Paris to the status of royal capital city. The Ile de France,
with Paris at its center, had gradually over the years developed into the nucleus of the future French nation, and it
radiated outward about a hundred miles, with radii extending
toward Chartres, Beauvais, Rheims, Amiens, Bourges, and
Rouen, cathedral cities all.[20] About one hundred and fifty
French cathedrals were erected in the first half of the thirteenth century.[21] By the middle of the thirteenth century
Paris, a fortress city of Roman lineage, had been transformed physically. Studded with churches, some old and
some new but all giving the impression of recent construc-
tion, the city appeared white and new.[22] Paris, its prestige enhanced by the noble figure of Saint Louis, by its
shrine of holy relics and its lofty cathedral, had become a
city of prayer. "Who can ever know the prayers from
which a Paris sky is woven, " mused the poet; "may not the
softness of certain evenings come from lost orisons, lost
as dusk gently falls?"[23]

The city of Paris was to become, when the University
of Paris had developed out of the Cathedral School of Notre
Dame and had gained renown for its faculty of theology, the
capital city of Christendom as well as the intellectual center

of Europe. The dominant structure of Paris, the ecclesiastical city, was Notre Dame Cathedral.

Notre Dame Cathedral

Silhouetted against the skyline of Paris looms the
gray mass of Notre Dame Cathedral. The cathedral can be
viewed from the left bank or from the Seine. Each leaves
a distinct impression. Viewed from the left bank, the structure seems to rise up like a mirage.[24] This east end of
the cathedral presents a fairylike appearance with its slender
flying buttresses and chapels, its gabled transepts, its delicate, frothy spire which rises three hundred feet over the
central crossing expressing in its upward reach toward infinity the love of man toward God.[25] Viewed from the Seine,
the striking impression given by the cathedral is that of a
fortress guarding the heart of the city: a foursquare building
held in suspension by a magnificent array of flying buttresses,
the great width of its façade, its climbing power culminating
in two massive spireless towers, expressing strength and
victory.[26] Reflected in the black river, Notre Dame Cathedral floats, swings at anchor, a stately galleon.[27] The view
of the cathedral in its island setting suggests the image popular in early medieval times in which a church was compared
to a ship steering for harbor. In this ship, which the church
symbolized, the faithful were borne safely over the sea of
life to the haven of eternity.[28] Haven of individual destinies,
Notre Dame Cathedral has endured through the centuries,
victory written in every monumental detail: in its walls,
erect and unconquerable; its massive west front, a statement
of broad and lifting strength; its spireless towers, like un-
fulfilled aspirations. The message of Notre Dame Cathedral
is ever old, ever new: "My shoulders are broad; they will
sustain you."[29]

The cross shape of Notre Dame Cathedral and its
orientation toward the east follow a set of conventions which
religious art had been developing for centuries. In the plan
of the cathedral (1163-c1235), concentration and centralization are the significant features.[30] Its five-aisled design is
found only in major ecclesiastical establishments. The
building consists of a choir and a circular apse, a short
transept--that is, the arms that project at right angles to
the building--and a nave flanked by double aisles and square
chapels. The five aisles of the plan and the wealth of vistas
provided by the double side aisles as they encircle the choir

provide a sense of richness.[31] The structure is four hundred
and twenty-seven feet long, one hundred and fifty-seven feet
wide, and its foundations reach thirty feet below the ground.[32]
A massive retaining wall runs beneath the entire perimeter
of the monument. The heavy blocks of stone, although below
the surface and never meant to be seen, were trimmed as
carefully as any of the visible masonry above, setting a tone
of integrity for the entire structure. Behind the retaining
wall is an immovable mass of filling: flint, hewn stone, ce-
ment, as well as the wreckage of the Carolingian and Merovingian basilicas and the deep remains of the Gallo-Roman
city, its rampart and its pagan altars.[33]

High at the ends of the transepts, which are stubby
and do not protrude much, and along the upper clerestory
elevation are the stained glass windows. Their glow relieves
the somber majesty of the exterior's gray walls, and the
flow of light through them adds the dimension of color to
etherealize the interior space. Three currents of colored
light descend from the southern, western, and northern rose
windows down through the tall pointed arches to rest upon
the heart of the cross.[34]

The majestic western façade, with its square front
and pronounced verticals and horizontals, is classical in its
simplicity. What makes this the façade of all façades,
wrote Temko, is the complexity of the composition and the
resulting simplicity of the over-all effect.[35] The solid base
from which the façade rises provides the supporting element.
One hundred and thirty-five feet in width, one hundred and
forty-one feet in height, the façade is not quite a perfect
square, although scholars believed that a true square would
have given the illusion of greater width than height. The
towers convert the square into a rectangle. To the summit
of the towers the façade is two hundred and seven feet,
which is equivalent to a twenty-odd-story of modern con-
struction.[36] The principle of regular divisions gives the
façade its appearance of stability. The four buttresses rising from three sculptured portals divide the façade into
three vertical elements. The three major horizontal elements are the base, the rose window, and the towers. Each
level is marked by the use of galleries. Over the portals
stretches the gallery of kings with its fifty-six sturdy colonnettes, as heavy and serious as the wall beneath, marking
the façade with a horizontal line of force.[37] Over the central portal is the rose window, the center of the entire composition, forty-two feet in diameter, flanked by high double

windows which repeat the portals.[38] Stretching across the
façade above the rose window is the pierced arcaded gallery
whose slender colonnettes stand sixteen feet high, twice the
height of the gallery of kings, but less than a foot in diameter. This gallery leads into the towers. The spireless
towers, which have high pointed openings, crown the western
façade.[39]

The three portals of Saint Anne, the Last Judgment,
and the Virgin are deeply recessed, with successive encircl-
ing tiers of statued niches adorned with fine early Gothic
sculpture. The sculpture of the central portal, which is
taller and wider than those on either side, illustrates the
Last Judgment. The most impressive figure is that of the
Christ, full of compassion and majesty. Angels rest in the
arches above, and below are scenes of the Resurrection,
the separation of the blessed and the damned, while on the
sides of the portal appear the apostles. Twelve virtues are
placed at eye level above their corresponding vices, and the
riders of the Apocalypse are depicted as reminders of the
terror that will accompany the Second Coming.[40] The portals on each side of the central one are dedicated to the Virgin. The southern portal, the earliest door of the façade,
presents the Virgin in Majesty.[41] The remaining space is
consecrated to the history of Anne and Joachim and the birth
of their child, Mary. The story has given the name Portail
Sainte-Anne to the portal, although technically it is the Portail de la Vierge.[42] The northern portal, although slightly
smaller than the southern, has a gable. The subject of
this portal is the death and resurrection of the Virgin and
of her coronation. Below this appear scenes depicting the
occupations of the various months and the corresponding
signs of the zodiac.[43] The complexity of the composition on
this northern portal makes it inexplicable without the Golden
Legend, an anthology by Jacobus de Voragine, representing
anonymous oral legends which had, like their intricate manuscript illuminations, waited centuries to find visual representation in the portals and stained glass windows of the
Middle Ages. At the time that they were making their appearance in stone and glass, they were being collected and
written down by Jacobus de Voragine.[44]

All of these elements of the western façade have been
tied into a firm unity. The gallery of kings connects the
vertical and horizontal elements, and the upper arcaded gallery connects the body of the cathedral with the towers. The
elevation to three stories adds a quality of nobility. These

parts combine to form an harmonious, simple, and grace-
fully proportioned whole.[45] The design of the powerful west
front, Fletcher observed, is peculiarly suitable to the flat
island site from which it rises alone in its impressiveness.[46]
Although on one of the portals the dedication of the cathedral
is commemorated, showing King Louis VII kneeling opposite
Bishop Maurice de Sully, Notre Dame is the cathedral of an
ecclesiastical city rather than a cathedral with royal associations.[47] At Notre Dame Cathedral Mary is the center of
all things. She appears at the high altar and again in a
fourteenth-century statue at the crossing of the transept.
Her glorification is the subject of two of the rose windows,
of a series of quatrefoil reliefs on the north façade, and of
four of the six portals. The proud figure of Mary, the only
standing figure at Notre Dame to survive the Middle Ages,
appears on the central post dividing the doorway on the
north transept.[48] She was placed here to rule the entrance
of the church, her image available to common touch and
common imagination, larger than life, but in the center of
it. As patroness of the Cathedral of Notre Dame, the Virgin is a divinity of earth.[49] Notre Dame is the church of
the Virgin. Her air of simple nobility is related to the
monumental quality of the cathedral apparent in its plan, its
height, and its massive west front.

    Notre Dame Cathedral was built on a spot hallowed
from time immemorial, first as a place for the worship of
Celtic gods and goddesses, followed by the worship of Roman
deities and the erection of a temple with its altar raised to
Jupiter by the rivermen of Paris under the reign of Tiberi-
us; with Christianity came the cult of saints, the cult of
relics, and the cult of Mary.[50] In early medieval times the
space in front of the cathedral represented Paradise, and
the Latin form of the word, Paradisus, became corrupted
into paravisus, from which "parvis" was derived. This was
the place where mystery and miracle plays were given, and
in later times it was used as a stage by lay players and the
famous minstrels of Notre Dame. It became the campus of
the Cathedral School of Notre Dame out of which the University of Paris grew, and bookstalls were set up in front of
the cathedral. Here in this Place du Parvis, as noted above,
the brass compass star Kilomètre Zéro is to be found, marking the point from which everything begins. Notre Dame
Cathedral symbolizes the medieval achievement whereby the
long pathway of Latin genius merged into the Via Sacra of
the Cross.[51]

"Whatever the practical needs of the medieval town, "
wrote Mumford, "it was above all things, in its busy turbu-
lent life, a stage for the ceremonies of the Church. "[52] The
main purpose of this community was the living of a Christian
life and the worship and glorification of God. [53] The Christian conception of life, with its affirmation of suffering and
its readiness to give aid, brought into existence agencies for
which there is no evidence in earlier urban civilizations, and
at no point were these urban institutions separated from the
Church. [54] The hospital, the hospice, the almshouse, the
leprosarium, the institution for the aged found their place in
the design of the city in addition to religious architecture as
the visible symbols of this purpose.

Notes

1. "Paris, " op. cit., p. 286.

2. Fremantle and others, op. cit., p. 31.

3. "Paris, " op. cit., p. 286.

4. Ehrlich, op. cit., p. 172.

5. "Paris, " op. cit., p. 286.

6. Douglas, op. cit., p. 188.

7. "Paris, " op. cit., p. 288.

8. Douglas, op. cit., p. 188.

9. Laffont, op. cit., p. 40.

10. "Paris, " op. cit., p. 286.

11. Saalman, op. cit., pp. 38-39.

12. "Louis IX, " op. cit., p. 414.

13. Ehrlich, op. cit., p. 10.

14. Fletcher, op. cit., p. 474.

15. Temko, op. cit., p. 67.

16. Laffont, op. cit., p. 34.

17. "Paris," op. cit., p. 288.

18. Laffont, op. cit., p. 40.

19. Ibid., p. 44.

20. William Fleming, Arts and Ideas (third edition; New
     York: Holt, Rinehart and Winston, Inc., 1968),
     p. 181.

21. Fletcher, op. cit., p. 478.

22. Douglas, op. cit., p. 188.

23. Laffont, op. cit., p. 44.

24. E. H. Gombrich, The Story of Art (New York: Phaidon
     Publishers, Inc., 1951), p. 132.

25. Fletcher, op. cit., p. 481.

26. Temko, op. cit., p. 178.

27. "Paris," op. cit., p. 290, Plate I.

28. Helen Gardner, Art Through the Ages (fourth edition;
     New York: Harcourt, Brace and Company, 1959),
     p. 193.

29. Laffont, op. cit., p. 36.

30. Fletcher, op. cit., p. 481.

31. Ann Mitchell, Cathedrals of Europe (Great Buildings of
     the World Series. Feltham, Middlesex: Paul Ham-
     lyn, 1968), p. 57.

32. Laffont, op. cit., p. 34.

33. Temko, op. cit., pp. 126-27.

34. Ibid., p. 248.

35. Ibid., p. 183.

36. Ibid., pp. 180-81.

37. Ibid., pp. 181-82.

38. Fletcher, op. cit., p. 481.

39. Temko, op. cit., p. 185.

40. Mitchell, op. cit., p. 63.

41. Temko, op. cit., p. 190.

42. Mitchell, op. cit., p. 63.

43. Ibid.

44. Temko, op. cit., pp. 196-97.

45. Mitchell, op. cit., p. 57.

46. Fletcher, op. cit., p. 481.

47. Mitchell, op. cit., pp. 53-54.

48. Ibid., pp. 63-64.

49. Temko, op. cit., p. 203.

50. Ehrlich, op. cit., p. 172.

51. Douglas, op. cit., p. 187.

52. Mumford, op. cit., p. 277.

53. Ibid., p. 267.

54. Ibid.

Chapter 4

PARIS: THE UNIVERSITY CITY

Notre Dame Cathedral, Sainte-Chapelle, the Louvre, Les Halles: these structures represent the physical expression of secular and sacred power, a combination of creativity and control. The history of Paris was reflected in the lives of men who dominated the city through the ages. Kings and churchmen whose lives have become part of the material of history had stood face to face with momentous problems and had made momentous decisions which may be seen in historical perspective in all their difficulty and in all their grandeur. Their lives and the labors they undertook were translated into the structures they erected. It is in the physical structures of the city that past events, decisions made long ago, values planned out in orderly fashion and achieved, remain alive. The translation of personal choices into urban structures is one of the prime functions of the city.[1]

With the rise of Paris as a capital city under the first Capet, many functions that had been scattered and unorganized were brought together within the precincts of the Ile de la Cité. In bringing together and welding into a visible unity shrine, market, fortress, the city of Paris enlarged all the dimensions of life. All aspects of life were inseparably intermingled. Paris by its very form as a walled island city held together through the centuries these various forces, intensified their internal reactions, and raised the whole level of the achievement of its inhabitants.

The city of Paris as an island stronghold with the Seine as its moat offered to its society safety from attack and from natural dangers; social stability and cultural cohesion; the free exchange of ideas, techniques, tastes. The city offered personal liberty: "city air makes free" went an old saying, and it was generally true in Paris as in other medieval cities that town residence of a year and a day relieved the serf of all manorial obligations.[2] As a marketing center, the city spread out many goods for choosing.

41

The city of Paris offered, too, a number of other opportunities to make choices, to pursue distant and difficult goals,
for the very growth of the city depended upon bringing in
food, raw materials, skills, from other communities. Creative ideas also found their way into the city along the trade-
ways, and these ideas were cross-fertilized in the city.

By a responsive act of choice, people increasingly
sought out the city and became part of it by willing adoption
and participation. Fresh human opportunities as well as
security from physical dangers drew people from farther re-
gions into the capital city of the Capetians. Different racial
stocks, different cultures, different technological traditions,
different languages came together and intermingled. The
stranger, the outsider, the traveler, the trader, the refugee,
the slave, the invading enemy; the peasant, the artisan, the
cleric, the serf, the noble, the knight, the merchant; all
have had a part at each stage of the development of Paris.
These were the new inhabitants of the capital city. The urban pattern so woven was all the richer in texture because
of the varied threads that formed it. In bringing people
from the most distant parts of its hinterland into the same
milieu, the city of Paris increased in numbers. With the
concentration of population upon the island, the number of
people with specialized knowledge increased; and the greater
the population, the greater the expectation that creative
people would be included among them.

Not merely did each special group find more of its
own kind in the city, but each could discover in the give
and take of daily intercourse a wealth of human potentialities.
City air also made men free in the sense of providing the
environment for the creation of an original personality. The
city produced people with original minds due to the decrease
in the pressure for conformity that goes with size: unusual
behavior was not so conspicuous in the heterogeneity of
Parisian populations. Thus the city became a special environment for the making of persons: human beings were
more ready to transcend the claims of custom, more capable
of assimilating old values and creating new ones, of making
decisions and taking new directions, than people in a provincial area. The city became the agent for discrimination
and comparative evaluation, not merely because it spread
out so many goods for choosing, but because it created
minds of large range capable of coping with them.[3] These
minds, by the very closeness of urban communication, by
the stimulus from other minds needed to help each mind find

itself, would be open to a far greater variety of challenges
and suggestions than appeared in a smaller community. It
is in the city and only in the city on an effective scale with
sufficient continuity, Mumford pointed out, that these inter-
actions and transactions, proposals and responses, take
place.[4] Both stability and constant creativity are needed,
and that combination was the supreme gift of the city. The
city was the medium through which people and ideas were
brought together.

By providing the challenge and protection of an appreciative environment and the fellowship of other great minds
and personalities, the city became the agent of man's transformation, the organ for the fullest expression of personality.
Out of the functions and processes of the city arose a higher
capacity for cooperation and a widening of the area of communication and emotional communion. From these emerged
new purposes, no longer attached to the original needs that
brought the city into existence.[5] Creative individuals were
attracted into the Ile de la Cité. Within the city the human
life and energy of the community, after providing for society's
needs, were translated into art forms.

One of the principal functions of the city, as Mumford saw them, is the making and remaking of selves.[6]
Each urban period in any generation provides a number of
new roles and a diversity of new potentialities which bring
about corresponding changes in laws, manners, moral eval-
uations, costume, architecture. Finally, they transform the
city as a living whole.[7] They change the character of the
city. Such individuation of character goes along with the
development of other higher functions, for not only is the
intelligence quickened, but the feelings are tempered and
emotions are refined and disciplined by their constant interplay with those of other men against a setting of art. By
action and participation, by detachment and reflection, urban
man may give to a larger portion of life the benefit of a
continued play of collective mind and spirit. What began as
an outer struggle against the hostile forces which threatened
the city and a fulfillment of the needs that brought the city
into existence culminated in an inner drama, the human
drama, whose resolution is a more intimate self-understand-
ing and a richer inner development. Out of the ritual and
the dramatic action in all their forms emerged the human
dialogue. Mumford believed that perhaps the best definition
of the city in its higher aspects is to say that it is a place
designed to offer the widest facilities for significant conver-

sation. The dialogue, Mumford further pointed out, is one
of the ultimate expressions of life in the city. [8]

The dialogue was not a part of the original function of
the city, but was made possible by the inclusion of human
diversities within the confines of the city. Only where opposition is tolerated and differences are valued can struggle be
transmuted into dialectic. In its inner economy, therefore,
the city is a place that promotes mental war. [9] To overlook
the place of dialectic in the polis, Mumford stated, is to
overlook the city's main function: "the enlargement in human consciousness of the drama of life itself, through whose
enactment existence discloses fresh meanings, not given by
any momentary analysis or repetitious statistical order."[10]

The city of Paris in its Golden Age was the city of
Philip Augustus and of Louis the Saint, the greatest of the
medieval French kings; and it was the city of the Louvre,
of Sainte-Chapelle, of Notre Dame Cathedral, of Les Halles.
It was also the city of dialectic, of the University of Paris,
of Abelard, of Abelard's followers. The combination of
these characteristics made Paris in the thirteenth century a
unique city, widely representative of the civilization of the
age and yet at the same time intensely individual.

The city performs the important function of materiali-
zation, for buildings speak and act no less than the people
who inhabit them. The city also transmits a representative
portion of a culture in human patterns, for the single individual is related to his community, defined by the community and defining it in turn. [11] The ability to transmit in human patterns a representative portion of a culture, wrote
Mumford, is the great mark of the city: this is the condition for encouraging the fullest expression of human capacities and potentialities.[12]

The city of Paris in the fourth and fifth decades of
the twelfth century provided the appreciative environment and
the fellowship of great minds which attracted into its precincts several geniuses within a single creative generation
and connected their most vital work to one center of civilization. Five masters of thought and feeling crossed one
another's paths along the Seine, and among them they dominate and represent every aspect of cultural change in the
period. These five giants are Abbot Suger, Otto of Freising,
Saint Bernard, Abelard, and John of Salisbury. The subsequent history of medieval thought, Cantor observed, could be

viewed with considerable plausibility as the working out of
their rich cultural legacy.[13] The achievements of these men,
each guided by his own high ideals and capable of willing the
realization of those ideals, left their mark upon the history
of the time, for these were men who dared and who achieved
because they took themselves and their ideals seriously.[14]
Paris provided the setting for the human drama, for at this
period of its history it was the vital center of an emerging
new cultural era. The human catalyst who generated the
change was Abelard. Of the five giants, the focus of the
following discussion centers upon Abelard.

        The study of dialectic in Paris advanced under Abe-
lard. "Dialectic, " which will be discussed more fully within
the context of teaching methods, derives from the Greek
word meaning discourse, or the art of debate.[15] Abelard's
views on theology and reason undermined the structure of
early medieval thought.[16] If not the first, Abelard was at
least the one with the most direct and far-reaching influence
who introduced dialectic into theology and reason into authority. Thus, by creating a new philosophical point of view,
he broke away from the traditional passive transmission of
the beliefs and dialectic accepted by the schools of theology
and introduced the principle of free intellectual inquiry,[17]
establishing a precedent of inestimable value to later generations. Outstanding contemporaries who found the new dialectical methods unacceptable presented alternative systems
of thought, but this did not stem the intellectual upheaval of
the time; it only added other facets to it, enriching and in-
tensifying its impact. These other approaches which were
offered helped to make the intellectual expansion of the
twelfth century a more comprehensive and complex movement, affecting all important aspects of higher culture, and
helped to increase the variety and magnitude of the problems
with which later generations of medieval thinkers had to
deal.[18]

        Abelard was an urban personality. His iconoclasm
and individualism reflected the fact that he was an urban
man.[19] The city of Paris provided the creative environment,
the stimulation of other great minds, the sufficient diversity
and competition which brought the performers in the human
drama to the highest pitch of intensely conscious participation. By action and participation, Abelard, his feelings and
emotions refined and disciplined by their constant interplay
with those of other men against a setting of art, gave to a
larger portion of life the benefit of a continued play of the

collective mind and spirit.   If Abelard had not towered above
contemporary philosophers, and if he had not been an aggres-
sive and unusual person with a great following among the
students, his moderate Nominalism would not have attracted
much attention.   As the most outstanding teacher of his day,
as both the most brilliant mind and the most forceful personality in the new schools, his opinions were bound to be influential.[20]   Although Abelard's doctrine was inevitably out-
moded by the impact on Western thought of Greek and also
to some extent of Arabic philosophy, he was, nevertheless,
the most important spokesman of the movement away from
the Platonic realism which had characterized the thought-
world of the early Middle Ages, and the next two centuries
of Christian thought were devoted to struggling with the implications of this intellectual revolution.[21]

Abelard translated his ideas, his decisions, his values,
his personal choices into no lasting physical structure, but
he left his intellectual tracks all around the banks of the
Seine, and the spirit which still broods over the university
hill of Sainte-Geneviève owes much to Abelard.[22]   He left
his mark upon the city of Paris, for at the beginning of the
twelfth century the Capetian capital on the Ile de la Cité became the capital of logic in France.[23]   The two later periods
of medieval intellectual development, between 1240 and 1270
and between 1300 and 1325, were concerned with meeting the
challenge of ideas and emotions which the great twelfth-century leaders imparted into the mainstream of medieval
thought.   Once the logical method had become general and
France had imposed its pattern of thought upon neighboring
nations, the capital city of logic was destined to become the
intellectual capital of Europe.[24]

Abelard, for the purposes of this study, is regarded
as one of the makers of Paris, the university city.   Background material for the above preview of Abelard is presented within the context of the cultural change which marked
the period from the early decades of the twelfth century to
about 1300, a period in which medieval culture took new directions.   The intellectual movement of the twelfth century
created something new, and this creativity deeply affected
all aspects of social life in which some intellectual endeavor
was required, a movement as broad and complex as medieval
civilization itself.[25]   Some of the forces which accelerated
medieval cultural change are presented in the following discussion.

During the tenth and eleventh centuries the world of
the early Capets, which was establishing the foundations of
social order, had to concern itself with the immediate problems of defense and provision of food and clothing and other
necessities for society and could not release its best minds
for speculative thinking.[26]   The combination of a favorable
environment and a new world view brought about a period of
cultural change: Paris began to respond to new stimuli.
The religious fervor of the Crusades, which brought contacts
with other peoples; technological progress, which released
creative minds from routine tasks; the expansion of trade
and commerce, which brought new ideas as well as new
materials; the growth of cities, which concentrated culture
in the cities; political unity, which brought a more ordered
society; a geographical location at the crossroads of medieval Europe, which favored the creation of a synthesis of
culture--these were some of the external forces charging
the atmosphere of Paris in the period under consideration.
Deeper influences were also being felt, particularly in the
arts and letters, giving them new vigor.   Some of these influences were the change in religious feeling, classical works,
Arabic and Greek treatises, and the awakening of an intellectual curiosity.   In order to better understand the thoughts of
the scholars of this period whose lives were influential in effecting the growth of the University of Paris, it is useful to
know something of the atmosphere within which this development took place.   Since this is a huge problem, the discussion here is limited to certain aspects of the subject.   After
presenting a general impression of the spirit of the times as
it was characterized by the energetic flux vibrating through
the city of Paris during this period, and the convergence of
certain of these forces culminating in the growth of the University of Paris followed by a synthesis of culture in the
thirteenth century, the discussion continues in broad outline
with an examination of teaching methods at the University of
Paris as they pertained to scientific method, the effect of
the invention of printing upon these methods of teaching and
also upon the volume of book production, and the concomitant
effect of this volume production upon the physical expansion
of the city of Paris.

The Crusades brought upheaval to the structure of
medieval society and the patterns of medieval life.   Religious
feeling underwent change.   Seclusion in a spiritual fortress
was no longer the ideal.   The age of faith was on the march
in answer to the appeal of Urban II in 1095 to create a cru-
sading force.   The Holy Land had taken on a significance

more usually associated with the veneration of relics, and
relics were precious. [27] The Crusades held forth the inspira-
tional promise of a direct pathway to heaven; merely to see
the earthly Jerusalem was to catch a glimpse of the Heavenly City toward which all men strove. As soldiers of Christ,
most nobles assumed that the bearing of arms was to be
viewed as a religious experience, to which the cross on
each shoulder gave visible witness, and the age of chivalry
had arrived. Returning crusaders found kinship with the
Knights of the Round Table, and the quest for the Grail
seemed to them a projection of their own adventures. [28] The
mass of mankind found a way to express devotion by the worship of Mary, who as a mortal woman and a mother, seemed
nearer to them than either the Father or the Son, less remote and more accessible than the formalized Trinity of official Christianity. Medieval man in general accepted the
Trinity without proofs, as the Church advised. The Trinity
is not found in the triple portal of Notre Dame; the place
that belonged theoretically to the Father and the Holy Ghost
is taken by the Virgin. [29] It was believed that Mary would
better understand human problems and act as intercessor with
her Son. Mariolatry brought with it the belief that earthly
women as sisters of Mary were deserving of particular consideration, while returning crusaders, insofar as their wan-
derings had exposed them to the compelling majesty of Mary,
were prepared to elevate the status of woman and to pro-
claim her virtues. [30] The true importance of the Crusades
lay in the forces they generated, forces that had a far-
reaching effect on every facet of European life. They demonstrated that the West had achieved a dynamic economic, political, and military vigor. Through contact with the East,
the community of Western Europe had been stimulated by a
new culture, a culture which it rapidly proceeded to surpass.
With the emergence of some degree of stability, these contacts opened the way for the revival of learning. [31]

    The growth of cities contributed to the change in re-
ligious feeling. Towns were a catalyst for religious ferment. In the twelfth-century world of the Capets which was
growing more ordered, wealthy, populated, literate, many
were beginning to reflect upon their beliefs; and although
they continued to believe, they could no longer believe with
naive or unthinking acceptance. Towns were man-made,
while the countryside was not. The city environment thus
tended to encourage the belief that prosperity in business affairs depended almost entirely upon personal qualities such
as intelligence, energy, resourcefulness. Towns seemed,

too, more man-centered than the countryside. Urban man,
unlike the peasant whose harvest was constantly threatened
by climatic catastrophes, could seldom blame droughts,
blights, or other natural disasters for his failures. If he
failed, he could find the cause only in his own shortcomings,
just as his successes were the natural outcome of his abili-
ties. For the city bourgeois, the fear of divine intervention
had receded; and as an urban man, he saw little danger in
enjoying the worldly pleasures of this life without worrying
overmuch about the spiritual consequences. [32]

     While the middle-class bourgeois found his place and
his political organization within the guild system, the un-
trained and illiterate serf who became the urban worker
formed a strata of the starving and hopeless. The expression of this hopelessness was, typically, religious heresy,
a questioning of the underlying bases of the existing society.
Late medieval society's answer to this challenge, which
arose from the growth of the city and the gradual dissolu-
tion of the feudal system, was the mendicant orders. [33] A
desire to return to the simple, humble way of life of the
original disciples led to the establishment of the orders of
friars. Franciscans, Dominicans, Carmelites, and others
devoted their lives to simple pastoral work, to teaching,
and to living in poverty. Acceptance of the world with all
its needs, which had replaced the monastic ideal, encouraged
the lay virtues of wisdom, strength, justice and well-doing.[34]
When the friars of the mendicant orders arrived in medieval
Paris in the early thirteenth century, they found a city seeth-
ing with the social, political, religious and intellectual ferment of a society in rapid evolution. The space within the
old urban core was already filled with the cathedral, the
parish churches, the towers and houses of the urban nobility
and the bourgeois patricians. [35] The left bank of the city,
where the University of Paris or the Latin Quarter was to
be located, was still rural, with its schools arising amid
the vines and wheatfields, even after the wall was erected
by Philip Augustus around 1209. While the Rue Saint-Jacques,
the main through street, was lined with houses, the less de-
sirable areas around the walls remained unsettled. This is
where the Dominican order of Jacobins and the Franciscan
Cordeliers established themselves in the early decades of
the thirteenth century. The Servites found their place along
the wall on the right bank at the very edge of the commercial center, while the Carmelites remained outside the walls
in the faubourg of Saint Paul. The Carthusians settled there
in 1259. Since the mass of unfortunates was both figuratively

and literally living on the periphery of medieval urban society, and since the objectives of the mendicant orders could
be accomplished only by men prepared to live among those
unfortunates, the place, shape and scale of the mendicant
convents and churches were determined by this reality. The
mendicant orders were therefore urban-oriented.[36] The left
bank was thus the domain of the Church, and it is within the
atmosphere of this community on the left bank that the University of Paris developed.

While mastery of the Biblical patristic tradition of
the early Middle Ages could satisfy the spiritual needs of
neither the middle-class bourgeois nor the less fortunate
serf, neither could it satisfy the best minds of the time.
This tradition of the existence of God was taught much as
Archbishop Hildebert described it in the eleventh century:

> God is over all things, under all things; outside
> all, inside all; within but not enclosed; without but
> not excluded; above but not raised up; below but
> not depressed; wholly above, presiding; wholly be-
> neath, sustaining; wholly without, embracing; whol-
> ly within, filling.[37]

The questing minds of the twelfth-century scholars reached
past this framework across silent centuries to explore Greek
philosophy and science. Classical works by Cicero and
Seneca, Plato and Aristotle were read and reread by twelfth-
century writers. Quotations from the classics and allusions
to the ancients were made by authors in romances, in theological treatises, in sermons. These writers handed on
their preoccupations and ideas to their followers.[38]

Men sought eagerly after all knowledge. Apart from
logic, whole tracts of metaphysical, moral, and natural
philosophy, and other subjects also, were unrepresented
among the classics. A rising number of Greek and Arabic
treatises was added to these classical works through the
work of Arabian scholars. Several centuries before the institution of the first universities in Christian Europe, a system of higher education had been effectively organized in
Baghdad, Alexandria, Cairo and Cordova, cities in contact
with Arabic culture.[39] Scholars from these schools, who
came from all over Europe, became the translators of Greek
and Arabic works into Latin. Translations were made of
works on philosophy, literature, medicine, mathematics, astronomy and astrology, as well as translations of the scien-

tific and geographical books of Galen, Hippocrates and Ptolemy. In medicine, the studies of Avicenna (d. 1027), the most famous being his Canon, were translated. The doctrines of Aristotle were made known to the philosophers of Paris by means of the lecturers at Cordova, and early in the thirteenth century the commentaries of Averroës (d. 1198) on Aristotle's philosophy were translated into Latin.[40] By the thirteenth century, however, more reliable translations of Aristotle were being made directly from the Greek instead of by way of Arabic versions, although the commentaries of the Arabic philosophers continued to be influential.[41]

The number of works recovered is large. One list, for example, drawn by the pupils of one of these translators called Gerard of Cremona, who died in Toledo in 1187, runs to seventy-one works.[42] Latin translations of Arabic works were especially significant because the Arabs revived and expanded the scientific and rational attitude of Greece, to which they added their own attainments, thus introducing the superior Arabic learning on mathematics, science and medicine to the West. Geographical works, which had gained in interest from the travels of missionaries in Asia, revealed the diversity of the world; medical, botanical and zoological treatises drew attention to flora and fauna, physics and physiology; and Aristotle became the authority in European thought in the twelfth and thirteenth centuries. Such translations contributed to intellectual activity and influenced curricula for the remainder of the Middle Ages.[43] The intellectual vigor of the East was thus transmitted to the West, but it remained for the thirteenth century and Saint Thomas Aquinas to assimilate this new Greek and Arabic knowledge with Christianity.

By 1200, towns and their trade were well established and thriving. Through their commerce they reached out to all parts of the known earth, widening man's understanding and deepening his appreciation for the universality of the human condition. The expansion of trade and commerce, the development of technology, the concentration of culture in the cities--all of these factors contributed to the increasing complexity of cities. New problems arose whose solution could no longer be supplied by the passive teachings of monastic or cathedral schools. By attracting creative individuals and by creating minds of large range capable of coping with urban diversity, the city became a catalyst for intellectual as well as religious ferment.[44]

With urban life came the beginning of the middle-
class tendency to regard education as the key to advancement.
Schooling was an urban phenomenon. Urban man knew that
unless he had the literacy to handle the problems of international commerce which required the ability to correspond
and to keep accounts, he could not compete in the marketplace. Education, however, did not end with completion of
the academic requirements. In their encounters at towns
and fairs, travelers and merchants from all over the world
exchanged ideas and cultural values, which helped to break
down the barriers of provincialism. [45]

Two influences of importance guided the thought of
the period: first, the traditional syllabus of studies reaching
back to classical times, discussed above; and, second, intellectual curiosity, that impulse to thought provided by the
practical difficulties of organized life whether secular or sacred. Without intellectual curiosity these influences would
have proven sterile; intellectual curiosity transformed the
syllabus of studies and made the difficulties of practical,
everyday life the starting point for the study of problems of
universal significance. [46]

At the beginning of the period under consideration,
education was a function of the monasteries and of bodies
such as the parish or other city churches. Toward the
middle of the twelfth century, when the left bank was still
rural and the roadless forest stood darkly beyond the crest
of the hill, the abbeys of the left bank--Saint-Germain-des-
Prés, Saint Victor, and Sainte-Geneviève--were storehouses
of wealth. Hundreds of serfs who lived in the villages that
were clustered beneath their walls worked the fields and did
chores within these walled lands. There were tasks which
kept these monastic communities constantly alive to the
world of learning, of which the serf was not unaware. The
tasks involved in the practice of the Christian religion--the
church services, the formulation of doctrine and the work of
church government, the maintenance of discipline--called for
a body of learning which penetrated every field of inquiry.
These activities, which included tasks such as writing the
necessary books for the elaboration of church services; the
writing of saints' lives, hymns, antiphons, lectionaries; the
setting of words to music, were a source of continuous intellectual effort. They provided great scope for learning,
and their performance created a stimulating intellectual environment. [47] Even the comparatively humble task of seeing
that the services began at the right time required careful

thought. At a time when there were no clocks and the times
of the services or routine tasks varied with the seasons, it
meant that the night watchman who communicated the information to the bell ringer had to know the names of the stars,
their courses, the times of their rising and setting, and the
difference between planets and fixed stars.[48] It was by performing these necessary tasks or merely living in an atmosphere where such tasks were performed that the common man,
as well as the cleric, maintained contact with the store of
ancient learning. The tasks involved in the practical difficulties of life in the monastery might well have occupied the
best talent of the monastery, but the illiterate serfs were
not unaffected. Leaving the monastic world and walking over
the Petit-Pont connecting the left bank with the Ile de la Cité,
which was surmounted by the houses of intellectuals, was
like passing through a street of the mind, where marvelous
talk could be heard in every doorway.[49] Much of this talk
in the middle of the twelfth century must surely have concerned a great man named Abelard and his questioning of the
church authorities.

The city of Paris was the medium through which common people and ideas were brought together. The great traditions embodied in religion, literature, history; expressed
in monuments, books, painting, music, architecture; served
by the other arts and sciences, made up a large part of the
core of medieval civilization. Knowledge about the intellectual products of the literate world was communicated to the
folk society by the illiterate serfs who had contacts with both
worlds; by minstrels, jongleurs, troubadours; by dramatic
performances and dances; by songs and proverbs; and then
they were related by parents and grandparents to children.
These oral traditions found visual representation in various
art forms. Images in tapestry, sculpture, and in stained
glass windows clothed ideas in human form. These art
forms described a way of life, and as such were the media
for those who shared that life to identify with one another as
members of a common civilization. Through the medium of
these art forms the highest conceptions of theologian and
scholar were communicated to some extent to the minds of
the humblest.[50]

The main purpose of the medieval city in Europe as a
collective structure, it has been noted, was the living of a
Christian life. The Church, aware of the power of art over
humble souls, tried through sculpture and stained glass to
instill into the faithful the full range of its teaching. For

the immense crowd of the illiterate whose only book was the
church, it was necessary to give visual representation to abstract thought. "These great churches, " wrote Mâle, "are
the most perfect known expression in art of the mind of an
epoch. "51 In the second half of the twelfth century while
the learned doctors were constructing their intellectual edi-
fice which was to become the University of Paris, the new
cathedral of Notre Dame was rising as its physical counterpart. On the western façade of Notre Dame Cathedral, the
whole philosophy of the age is displayed. Around the figure
of the Virgin are grouped the saints of the Old Testament,
the rhythmical sequence of the works of the months, and the
figures of the virtues and vices carved on the portals. The
illustrations from the Golden Legend on the north portal
taught the Christian something not only of life but of other
times and other countries and gave to the Middle Ages a dim
idea of history and geography, albeit in a distorted form as
in old maps. In his book, Notre Dame de Paris, Victor Hugo wrote: "In the Middle Ages men had no great thought
that they did not write down in stone. "52 This people's book
of stone, a precursor of the printed book, was gradually
rendered valueless by the introduction of printing into Paris.
As Victor Hugo expressed it, "The Gothic sun set behind the
colossal press at Mainz. "53 These various influences--the
tasks, the intellectual environment, the art forms, the ca-
thedral--contributed to stimulating intellectual curiosity
among the common people. Against a setting of art the intelligence was quickened, and a curiosity to know more was
born.

      Perhaps intellectual curiosity might best be observed
in the generation which matured about 1100. From the obscure parts of France, England, Italy, and even Germany,
young clerical scholars took to the roads, moving from place
to place to sit at the feet of some famous teacher whose reputation had penetrated into their homeland. Men as well as
boys traveled constantly, eager to learn, to inquire, to argue, to teach. Their restless intellectual quest for knowledge
shattered the framework of the Biblical patristic tradition
within which the masters of the earlier Middle Ages had
worked. 54

      With the twelfth century, intellectual curiosity and
self-confidence grew. Clerks became interested in the con-
formation of the globe; in the nature of air, water, fire; in
the movement of the winds; in the position of the stars, the
nature of animals, the growth of plants. Confidence and

faith in the power of reason grew to the point where reason
was applied universally to law; to politics; to jurists, philosophers, theologians; to music; to teaching methods. This
intellectual curiosity and self-confidence brought about a full-
er development of the European mentality. [55] The twelfth-
century world was no longer formless, subject to arbitrary
forces and supernatural powers, but a coherent, harmonious
unity governed by laws, intelligible to human reason. The
universe and humanity had a validity of their own. Such
ideas helped to strengthen culture and to confirm its direction. The twelfth century described man and his feelings,
nature and its wonders; the thirteenth century explained and
clarified, searched for common causes and principles. [56] No
one in 1100 or even 1140 could clearly perceive the recon-
struction of the Christian thought world which would result
from these new investigations.

The University of Paris

The beginning of the University of Paris and a prime
cause of its activity may be found, scholars believe, in that
period of creativity called by some the "Twelfth Century
Renaissance." Douglas points out that the beginnings of the
university movement in Paris derived directly from an
awakened curiosity stimulated by the presence of great teachers filled with ardor, and from the enthusiasm of a large
student body eager to learn, a tradition carried on without
interruption from the time of Abelard. [57] The most central
figure in the intellectual expansion of twelfth-century Europe
is Peter Abelard. Although the University of Paris even in
its most rudimentary state did not exist until a generation
after Abelard, he did help to inaugurate the intellectual movement out of which it grew.

Of the generation which came to maturity about 1100,
while some as the soldiers of God answered the call of Urban
II by joining the Christian crusade in the counter-offensive of
the West against the Moslems, others set off for the cathedral
schools to participate in the intellectual revolution. Among
the most brilliant of this new generation was Peter Abelard
(1079-1142). Son of a minor lord in Brittany south of the
Loire, a region known for its savage warriors but not particularly for its scholars and philosophers, Pierre du Pallet,
better known as Peter Abelard, early abandoned his inheri-
tance and his knightly career to become a scholar. Like so
many of the others, he wandered from one cathedral school

to another, studying with all the famous masters.[58]

There were things to be learned in northern France which satisfied intellectual aspirations far beyond the range of legal sciences or the requirements of monastic routine. Logic and grammar were subjects in which intellectual novelties and excitements were to be found.[59] Theologians in the eleventh century had begun to concern themselves for the first time since Saint Augustine with philosophical problems relating to theology. Augustine had assimilated and passed on to later ages much of Plato's thought. Based upon this work, the concern of eleventh- and twelfth-century thought was the fundamental nature of what scholars termed "universals" and "particulars."[60] The "realists," to put it briefly, were convinced that particulars could not be understood nor have any reality unless associated with and partaking of the nature of their general ideas or universals. Opposed to these realists were the "nominalists," who believed that universals had no real existence of themselves but were used merely to facilitate reference to abstract ideas; further, general ideas or universals were but names, the Latin nomina, from which the term "nominalists" was derived.[61]

The first exponent of the nominalist view was the theologian Roscellinus, under whom Abelard was later to study. Roscellinus stated that universals were not real or were not things, but were names. An ecclesiastical council compelled him to retract his statements in 1092.[62] The belief arose that intelligent appreciation of spiritual truth depended upon correct use of prescribed methods of argument, and dialectic was looked upon as the "science of sciences."[63]

The cathedral schools where masters were wont to teach were the rallying points of the intellectual movement. The Cathedral School of Chartres was a stronghold of classical learning. Fulbert, Bishop of Chartres from 1006 to 1028, had made that school the most vigorous in Europe. At the Cathedral School of Notre Dame, the scholars who had been licensed by the Bishop of Paris to teach in his school dealt with subjects which had no place in the circumscribed world of the monastery. Using the new intellectual tools of dialectic, these scholars were prepared to analyze and resolve the problems of Western thought.[64]

When William of Champeaux opened a school in the first decade of the twelfth century for the more advanced study of dialectic as an art at the Cathedral School of Notre Dame in

Paris--the earlier Notre Dame, not the present one begun in
1163--his classes were well attended. [65] He won renown as
a teacher of dialectic by defending the realist position. Abelard made his way to the new schools of philosophy and theology at Chartres and Paris, then to the school of dialectic
at Notre Dame. From the beginning, Abelard was recognized as an exceptionally brilliant student, and he became
an adept in dialectic, the favorite study. With his exceptional gifts, Abelard was soon the equal of his teacher. William
of Champeaux started from the ultimate substance, God, the
Universal; Abelard started from the opposite point, the atom,
the individual, the observed fact of experience. They came
to grips somewhere between these two points. Abelard won.
He so ably refuted the realist position of William of Champeaux that the hostility of the clerical authorities forced him
to resume his travels. [66]

Abelard decided to turn to theology; he accordingly
went to Laon to study under Anselm, the master famous in
that subject. At Laon he out-taught, out-argued and outraged
the master, and was summarily expelled. By this time,
however, his scholarly fame was great, and in 1115 he secured an official appointment as teacher of logic and theology
at the Cathedral School of Notre Dame. [67] The rise and fall
of Abelard at Paris was meteoric. A stimulating teacher
and thinker of the first order, he attracted students in large
numbers and became recognized as the leading scholar. In
Paris the love idyll with Héloïse, brilliant niece of Fulbert,
canon at Notre Dame, quickly turned into tragedy; his brilliant career ended. Abelard became a monk; Héloïse, a
nun. The rest of his life was a series of unhappy crises. [68]
Abelard became abbot of a Breton monastery, where he wrote
his autobiography, The History of My Calamities; but he soon
gave up the Breton monastery. He then entered the monastery of Saint Denis, where he was miserable. Abelard re-
turned to Paris to teach, and students flocked to hear him,
but his teachings were declared heretical by Saint Bernard. [69]

Saint Bernard of Clairvaux was a bitter opponent of
Peter Abelard. For him the truth could only be arrived at
through Christ. True wisdom consisted in seeking Him and
following Him, and the science to be taught above all others
in the schools was the knowledge of His love. Basically,
Bernard was a mystic, the mystic of the living God, the
God made man, and His mother the Virgin Mary. He was
in his time the foremost representative of mystical theology,
which had a great following. Bernard and Abelard were the

two leaders of popular opinion in France, and Bernard finally
succeeded in silencing Abelard. [70]

Denounced by Saint Bernard for publishing heretical
doctrines, Abelard was subsequently summoned before a
church council and forced to recant. Undaunted, Abelard
set out for Rome to appeal the decision to the Pope. He
fell ill en route; he died at Cluny in 1142; his body was re-
turned to Héloïse for burial. [71] The faces of Abelard and
Héloïse are brought together again in the statuary of a capital in the Palais de Justice. [72]

Abelard was unquestionably one of the greatest figures
in the intellectual history of Europe. He made contributions
of importance to philosophy, to theology, and particularly to
the study of dialectic. So notably did he contribute to the
advancement of dialectic that by the middle of the twelfth
century, John of Salisbury, who became Bishop of Chartres,
could say that all learned Paris had gone well-nigh mad in
its pursuit and practice. [73] While the indirect influence of
his teaching has yet to be assessed, the direct influence of
his writings was limited. Yet no other works of the early
twelfth century show the deep concern with a vast range of
problems or the critical attitude toward past and contemporary solutions which characterize the period. His extant
works fall into five groups: theological writings, philosophi-
co-theological writings, logical treatises, letters, and poeti-
cal compositions. [74] The best known of his works are his
autobiography, The History of My Calamities, and Sic et Non,
or Yes and No, a collection of apparently contrasting passages in the form of one hundred and fifty-eight questions on
dogma, which he answered with conflicting quotations from
the Scriptures, the Church Fathers, and the pagan classics,
but for which he offered no solutions. [75] As to the quantity
of production and the wide circulation of these writings, a
letter of Saint Bernard bears testimony to their great popularity:

> I would that his poisonous pages were still lying
> hid in bookcases, and not read at the cross-roads.
> His books fly abroad.... Over cities and castles
> darkness is cast instead of light.... His books
> have passed from nation to nation, and from one
> kingdom to another people.... It is his boast that
> his book has where [sic] to lay its head, even in the
> Roman curia. [76]

With the death of Abelard in 1142, the city of Paris,
although reportedly it had doubled in size under Louis VI,
who ruled from 1108 to 1138, was still small, but already
it had become the special home of what was most productive
in medieval civilization. The world was opening, enlarging,
discovering its capacities. [77]

The significance of Abelard's achievement for the purposes of this study rests upon his teaching experience, the
effect of its uniqueness upon teaching methods, upon the
commencement of the University of Paris, and upon the expansion of the city of Paris. In the year 1100 there was as
yet little to indicate that Paris was to be the capital of logic
in France, or the intellectual capital of Europe, or the home
of a great university. There were other schools established
in Paris at that time in the monasteries of Sainte-Geneviève,
Saint Victor, and Saint-Germain-des-Près, as well as at the
Cathedral of Notre Dame, but these schools were not particularly distinguished. The Cathedral School of Chartres, on the
other hand, had earned a brilliant reputation as early as the
end of the tenth century, and pupils were already beginning
to gather there from distant provinces. In the eleventh and
twelfth centuries Chartres was the finest school in Latin
Christendom. The masters of this school--Fulbert, "the
venerable Socrates"; the great Bishop Ivo; Gilbert Porretanus
--were counted among the greatest of the Middle Ages.
These masters, distinguished for their encyclopedic learning,
their respect for the ancients, their scorn for new methods
of teaching, had made the school of Chartres the refuge of
tradition. It is not surprising, therefore, to find the seven
liberal arts represented in sculpture on the Royal Portal or
in stained glass in the chapel of Saint Piat at Chartres Cathedral. The school of Laon, under the celebrated master
Anselm, "the light of France and of the world," was almost
as famous as that of Chartres and had been the leading
school of Christendom for nearly half a century. [78] Nevertheless, before the end of the twelfth century it was neither
Chartres nor Laon, but the Cathedral School of Notre Dame
in Paris that had developed into a university, and its early
schools and lecture rooms were located in the shadow of the
great cathedral on the Ile de la Cité.

One of the great educational changes of the period, then,
was the transference of general teaching from the monasteries to the cathedral schools, the essential difference being
that the former were rural and often isolated while the cathedral was by definition urban. Another great educational

change was the breaking away from the mere passive transmission of the beliefs and the timid dialectic accepted by
the schools of theology, referred to above, which made possible the development of the true university spirit of free intellectual inquiry. It was from the presence of Abelard in
Paris about the middle of the twelfth century, wrote Douglas,
from the disputes he stimulated, and above all from the
crowds of pupils he attracted that the University of Paris
took its origin, in spirit if not in form. [79]

Although Abelard was not the first teacher to attract
students to Paris, his personal qualities, his capabilities as
a teacher, and his great popularity stimulated much enthusiasm for learning among the students and attracted them in
large numbers to Paris.   Three qualities were outstanding,
according to the students who sat at his feet: clearness,
richness in imagery, and lightness of touch. [80]   Abelard
possessed great oral power: versatility, supported by a
rich voice; a thorough knowledge of the classics then available, and a retentive memory; an ease in manipulating his
knowledge, and a clearness of expression; a freedom from
excessive piety, and a productive imagination; a great knowledge of men, and a warmer interest in things human than in
things divine; a laughing contempt for authority, a charming
personality, a handsome appearance.   Abelard was a genius
of the first rank.   He impressed everyone he met by the
force of his personality and the power of his intellect.   His
study of classical literature enabled him to develop a style
which, added to his charm of voice and manner, made him
the best lecturer in Europe, and in an age when the high
cost of manuscripts and the time involved in copying them
by hand made books scarce items, the capabilities of a teacher were of the first importance. [81]

Abelard's capabilities as a teacher had a particular
significance in the twelfth century.   The masters and students
lived in an extremely competitive society.   If a lecturer's
mental and other qualities impressed his audience, he was
successful; if he appeared uninteresting and unimportant, he
would lose his students.   In Abelard's day, if the teacher
could not attract students he had nothing to fall back upon;
he lived entirely by his wits. [82]   No salaries were paid to
the teachers, and they had the right to teach for whatever
fees they could extract from whatever students they could
persuade to come to their lectures.   Since the students
themselves hired and paid the teachers, they also determined
the courses to be given.   Students, then, were a force to be

reckoned with since they might desert one master's classes for those of another. [83] A measure of Abelard's popularity with the students is indicated by the fact that in his period of self-exile in a monastery, the students sought him out and prevailed upon him to resume his lectures, although upon his return reviving fame brought renewed threats of persecution.

The unique circumstances of Abelard's academic world, the awe with which he was regarded by students who pondered his every word, his magnetic personality and charismatic personal qualities made a profound impression upon society and contributed to the growth of the university. His individualism was a precursor in twelfth-century society of the Renaissance with its emphasis upon the social importance of man. [84] In addition to this, or perhaps a part of the whole picture, is the exciting factor of Abelard's new approach to teaching methods. While his personal gifts gave him an immeasurable advantage over other teachers, the characteristic which most distinguished Abelard from his peers was his doubting and inquisitive mind. In sharp contrast with the typical medieval master, one of whom was Anselm of Bec, whose philosophy is stated in the words, "Nor do I seek to know that I believe, but I believe that I may know," Abelard's position is summed up in his famous statement, "For by doubting we come to inquiry, and by inquiring we perceive the truth. "[85]

Abelard's statement appeared in the prologue of his Sic et Non. The method of Sic et Non is the basic idea of Abelard's method of ordering his theological arguments. The one hundred and fifty-eight opinions of Sic et Non had been collected because, as mentioned above, they were to some extent contradictory; some could be explained in various ways and some not. When not, it was Abelard's belief that the best authority must then be taken. In any case, Abelard did not supply the answer, leaving the problem for the student to work out, but the student had first to realize that a doubt existed as to the proper answer. [86] Abelard's purpose was to apply logic to the inherited mass of patristic writings, to show where the truth of Christian doctrine really lay and so make faith consistent with reason and reflection. [87] Abelard emphasized the creative power of reason; he wanted to stimulate inquiry, which he believed to be the key to wisdom. Abelard also observed that many of the apparent contradictions might come from the use of the same word with different connotations by different writers, and

this observation is linked with his solution of the problem of
universals, his chief title to fame.   This theory of Abelard's
was important because it was original, and also because the
problem treated and the manner of treating it were strictly
philosophical; that is, the question was studied outside of any
theological context and its solution was arrived at by pure
logic.   One consequence of his method was that it provided
a precedent for the science of logic to be set up as independent study, free of metaphysics, since it took as its object
not beings but words. [88]

The method that Abelard introduced became the method
usually followed in theological works, one proof being its influence in the succeeding generation.   Peter Lombard (c1100-
1164), the disciple of Abelard who became Bishop of Paris
in 1159, collected in his Magister Sententiarum, or Book of
Sentences, different authorities pro and con, and then harmonized them by distinctions or inferences. [89]   The design of
Sentences was to place before the students in as strictly logical a form as practicable the views of the Church upon the
most difficult points in the Christian belief.   Logicians regarded this work as a storehouse of indisputable major premises on which they argued with renewed energy and with
great dialectical refinement.   Sentences was not so much
original in itself as it was progressive in its systematization,
the systematization being due to the method of Abelard.   This
work became the accepted textbook of theology for the later
Middle Ages. [90]   The influence of Abelard's method is also to
be noted in the Decretals, or decrees, of the monk Gratian,
entitled Concordantia Discordantium Canonum, dated about
1140. [91]   The weakness of canon law had been its lack of
systematic codification.   This work became the authority for
the schools of canon law. [92]   Saint Thomas Aquinas (1225?-
1274) lent his great prestige in the thirteenth century to Abelard's method in his unfinished masterpiece, Summa Theologiae, or Summary of Theology.   The method used in the
Summa was the dialectical one, presenting successively argument and counterargument.   Thomas Aquinas presented six
hundred and thirty-one basic questions and then attempted to
supply satisfactory answers by using canon law and syllogis-
tic reasoning.   When he found it impossible to supply a
good answer or to reconcile conflicting truths, he concluded
that the revealed truth must be accepted because it came
from God who was the Creator and the embodiment of all
truth. [93]   The Summa Theologiae of Saint Thomas Aquinas is
the classic achievement of the scholastic method.   Aquinas's
motivation is expressed in his own statement, "Grace does

not destroy Nature but it fulfills it, " and this standpoint
enabled him to use both reason and faith in his argument.
He used the concept of Natural Law to emphasize the participation of man by reason in the divine ordering of the universe. [94]   The thought of Aquinas, as recently as 1879, was
pronounced by Pope Leo XIII to be the foundation of official
Catholic philosophy. [95]

By progressing one step further than Abelard, by providing a solution to the problems after citing the quotations
pro and con, these scholars substituted a new authority, and
the result was wholly different from Abelard's method in Sic
et Non of throwing the discussion open without a solution.
Texts in favor, texts against, and resolution by logical reasoning, these are the bases of the scholastic method. [96]
"Scholasticism, " the name usually employed to denote the
most typical products of medieval thought, is a complex,
many-faceted subject, and it is used in this study only as it
relates to the influence of Abelard upon the stream of Western thought and its contribution to the development of the
scientific method.

It was through the long-range influence of Abelard's
method of teaching that "the theological school of Paris became the seminary of Christian Europe. "[97]   This new
method of instruction, concurrently with new material upon
which to exercise it, scholars believe, may well have had
its effect upon the development of cathedral schools into
universities in general, and in particular upon the development of the Cathedral School of Notre Dame into the University of Paris.   The influence of this new method also had a
far-reaching effect upon book production, for it continued
through the centuries.   During this time Paris remained the
center of theological instruction, and this in turn had an important effect in shaping the character of the earlier issues
of the Paris press, in the development of the city of Paris
into the capital of logic in France, and the intellectual capital of Europe.

Saint Bernard of Clairvaux, among others, saw in
Abelard's methods the very source of heresy. [98]   Saint Bernard rightly judged that the appeal to human reason implied
in this new method would be dangerous and likely to provoke
doubt, since reverence for the authority of the Church would
naturally be shaken when the students attempted to form their
own opinions.   So long as Abelard merely lectured, however,
he was not molested; only when he began to publish his the-

ology did the Church interfere.[99] The method of Abelard
comes into sharp focus when contrasted with the teaching
methods of Bernard of Chartres, a contemporary, as described by John of Salisbury. John of Salisbury, himself a
bishop of Chartres in the last years before his death in 1180,
was of a younger generation than Abelard, but his vivid account of his teacher provides some valuable insight as to
traditional methods of teaching. Bernard would dispense his
instructions to his hearers gradually, in a manner commen-
surate with their powers of assimilation, wrote John in the
twelfth century;[100] and in view of the fact that exercise both
strengthens and sharpens the mind, Bernard would bend
every effort to bring his students to imitate what they were
hearing; in some cases he would rely on exhortation, in
others he would resort to punishments, such as flogging.

A typical day in the life of a student at Paris in Abelard's time would begin when the cathedral bell of Notre
Dame rang out at five or six in the morning, inviting the
students to arise and greet the new day. From the neighboring houses, the industrious would pour into the streets,
making their way to bare lecture rooms, or sometimes to
classes held in the open. The master's beadle would spread
hay or straw on the floor or on the ground, then bring to
the raised platform the master's textbook in which the notes
of the lecture were written between the lines or around the
margins, and then he would retire to secure silence in the
adjoining streets. Sitting on the straw or occupying rows of
hard benches, one knee raised to serve as support for the
waxed tablet, the scholars would take notes. The lectures,
with some interruptions, went on for six or seven hours.
Students would then hurry home to commit their notes to
parchment while the light lasted. Meanwhile, grassy playing meadows beckoned along the banks of the Seine. The
curfew rang at nine.[101] Aspects of student life are illustrated in contemporary manuscripts, but vivid glimpses are
also reflected in large numbers of regulations. Again, in
contrast, the students of Abelard were not encouraged to
take notes even if they could afford the notebooks. They
listened and retained what they could remember. The one
valuable right the students of Abelard seem to have had was
the right of asking questions and even of disputing with the
master, provided they followed the correct form of dialectic.[102]

Another consequence of the uniqueness of Abelard's
teaching experience and the fame it brought to the city of

Paris was that it attracted students from all parts of Europe,
which in turn influenced the physical growth of the university
in two important ways: its expansion to the left bank, and
the development of the college system. The intellectual ferment of twelfth-century Paris was intense. Abelard had
brought into opposition against himself as the exponent of the
new Nominalism many of the most notable scholars of the
age, and their debates had attracted an ever-increasing audience. He became known as the "Master of Opposites."[103]
Some scholars report that Abelard's classes numbered about
five thousand students.[104] It is claimed, too, that when
Abelard set himself up as a teacher, some twenty or even
thirty thousand students poured into the city.[105]

An important reason for the very large numbers of
students is that the schools, which were actually embryonic
universities, were open to all free men without restriction,
as opposed to the more restricted ecclesiastical schools
which were under the rule of some religious order. Paris
was noted for the welcome it gave to men from all parts of
Europe.[106] Another reason is that these schools undertook
to supply not only the higher education which belongs to the
present university curriculum, but also the training now provided by gymnasia or high schools, which did not exist in
this early period. Therefore, membership included students
who were little more than boys, in age as well as in mental
development. On the other hand, these embryonic universities attracted mature students who were animated by the desire for knowledge; but more often they were attracted to
the intellectual environment of the city, since it was only in
an intellectual center that circles of scholars could be found,
or that books were available, or that intellectual activity
could be experienced.[107] Since Latin was the universal language of higher learning, and lectures as well as the written
works based upon them were also in Latin, students were
not hampered by language barriers and moved about easily
from school to school. This student body, whose multitude
almost surpassed that of the lay inhabitants, was cosmopolitan in character. In the thirteenth century the dominance of
this cosmopolitan society conferred upon the city in which
the University of Paris was established its own unique luster.
The Latin Quarter district has from this time forward remained unique in the world.[108]

The present location of the University of Paris on the
left bank of the Seine is also due to Abelard. The great
mass of students who came to study in Paris about 1100

thronged the cloister of Notre Dame, and the neighborhood of Notre Dame soon began to swarm with an enthusiastic, boisterous student body. As the fame of Abelard and of his scholastic tournaments spread, this small area became over-crowded. The need for more space and Abelard's own con-flicts with the ecclesiastical authorities led master and stu-dents to desire more independence from the officials of the cathedral. [109] The abbot of Sainte-Geneviève on the Mount was believed by some to have offered a suitable location on the left bank of the Seine. Granted permission by the Chap-ter of Notre Dame to cross the Petit-Pont and to teach out-side the confines of the cloister, Abelard and his followers migrated from the Cité and began to establish themselves in what has ever since been known as the Latin Quarter be-cause of the Latin language spoken there. [110]

Before the end of the twelfth century Paris was no longer a cathedral school, but a university. At first this "university" had no permanent quarters. There were no campus grounds, no ivied halls, no grassy malls; no labora-tories, no libraries, no equipment. Teachers and students were practically the only assets that the university in embryo possessed. [111] The world of these masters of the twelfth century, wrote Powicke, strangely resembled that of the knight errantry of the romances, a world of "libertines of the mind, " who moved about from one cathedral school to another, setting up schools for themselves and finding a measure of security in the friendship and patronage of great men, princes, abbots, and especially of bishops. [112] It was only by degrees that these masters combined into a commu-nity and that special buildings were constructed for their classwork. For a long time the teachers lived in separate houses on the island. If the new teacher's lodgings were adequate, he lectured there; but generally he had to hire a room. These lecture halls in the Latin Quarter came to be concentrated along the street called the Rue du Fouarre, the Street of Straw, so called because of the straw-covered streets and floors. By the thirteenth century, all the left bank was covered with quarters for students and rooms where the masters lectured. Not until the fifteenth century, however, did universities generally have buildings of their own. [113]

Among the student population were hundreds of needy who required assistance. Although medieval society was stratified and the increasing polarization of wealth had brought hostility and the intensification of class struggles, at the uni-

versity money and social prestige did not spell the difference
between success and failure. The important thing was intellectual achievement, and both Church and wealthy individuals
looked upon the support of worthy but poor students as a
necessary and pious work. Joining an order of friars was
one solution, but not for those who did not want to take the
vows. To provide for the needs of these students, the residential college came into being. [114]

The first college was the Collège des Dix-Huit, which
provided shelter for eighteen students, founded in 1180 by a
London vintner named Josse de Londres on his return from
a pilgrimage to Jerusalem. By the thirteenth century donors
began to establish colleges. In 1257 Robert de Sorbon, chap-
lain of Saint Louis, endowed a hall for theological students,
the Collège de Sorbonne. Originally intended for sixteen students of theology who were already Masters of Arts, it was
later enlarged by other benefactors to thirty-six, and in the
fourteenth century it became the home of the theological faculty. [115] Other residential colleges were rapidly founded,
and they began to climb the slopes of the left bank, finding
their place among the foundations of the mendicant friars.
The students relaxed, played and fought on the "Scholars'
Field" in the shadow of the walls of Saint-Germain-des-Près.
The left bank also became known simply as the University.
In the fourteenth century, the University of Paris had forty
colleges governed either by secular or religious communities,
and students representative of every country in Europe were
numbered among them. [116] By the sixteenth century about
seventy colleges had been founded. [117] Of these colleges, the
Collège des Dix-Huit and the Sorbonne illustrate the two
main types: the one intended for needy students, and the
other to maintain graduates in their long courses of theology
and canon law. The Sorbonne remains the oldest residential
college of which there is any record. Its close connection
with the faculty and the use of its hall for the disputations
of that body led to the word "Sorbonne" becoming a popular
term for the theological faculty of Paris; later it became the
synonym for the whole university, as it still is today. [118]
As an institution, this community of masters and students,
although it developed rapidly, did not secure its organization
until the early thirteenth century.

The University of Paris was a slow growth. It was
neither created, nor was it founded through any administrative action nor through lavish endowments. It just grew,
developing under special influences, as noted, out of the pre-

existing Cathedral School of Notre Dame. The physical separation of Abelard and his students from the cloister of
Notre Dame across the Seine to the left bank had a long-
range effect upon the general direction of medieval education.
The transfer of general teaching from the rural monastic
schools to the urban cathedral schools had been, as previously noted, one concomitant of the rise of cities. Inasmuch as
the transference of general teaching from the monks to the
secular clergy was to be one of the great educational changes
of the period, in that sense the rise to predominance of the
Cathedral School of Notre Dame over the other monastic
schools of Paris was the first step toward the later formation of the university.[119] The mere fact of the existence
outside of the cloister of Notre Dame of an important division of learning and of a great body of scholars contributed
to the trend toward the secularization of education. With
this physical transfer of the school premises went the transference of the responsibility for the preservation and the
development of the intellectual life of the community of Western Europe which the cathedral schools had taken over from
the monasteries. This change meant among other things that
the control and direction of education no longer rested with
the ecclesiastics, that the class of scholars was no longer
limited to the clerics, and that scholarly achievement was to
be sought in other directions than those marked out by the
Church.[120] The rise to leadership of the Notre Dame school
over notable rival cathedral schools established elsewhere,
attributable to the presence and teaching of Abelard at Paris
and the intellectual and social ferment which had been generated, scholars believe, may be regarded as the "true main-
spring of the University of Paris," which later was to achieve
an independent existence.[121]

    This change from cathedral school to university was
not without its impact upon society. Putnam observed that
it must have had a powerful effect upon the imagination of
communities which had for so many generations been ac-
customed to look to the Church as the source or as the interpreter of all knowledge. This is not to say that the
Church consciously abandoned the control of the education
which had rested in its hands for eight centuries. It is to
say that after the twelfth century the universities took the
lead in higher education, although the cathedral schools continued to instruct most of the candidates for the priesthood.
With the rise of the university, the general direction and
control of the work of higher education no longer rested with
ecclesiastics, but with laymen.[122] Heretical doctrines, or

what were believed to be heretical doctrines, were often
taught in university lecture rooms, but the Church maintained
the authority to interfere with such teaching. Although the
Church sponsored the establishment of these institutions of
higher learning, it was the university which henceforth was
the main carrier of theoretical and practical knowledge.[123]

To write the history of the University of Paris and
the development of the Latin Quarter would necessitate a
survey of almost the whole of medieval scholarship. The
organization of the University of Paris is of interest to this
study primarily because of its relationship to Abelard, to
teaching methods, to book production, and to the impact
which the prestige it bestowed had upon the city of Paris.
The purpose of the following discussion, therefore, is to
provide the necessary background for these subjects. The
main topics with which it is concerned are: the predominant
features of the organization of the University of Paris, the
development of the Latin Quarter, and the rise of Paris to
become the cultural center of Europe.

With both masters and students increasing in numbers,
it became necessary to institute organization. Students and
masters combined into communities or associations whose
organization followed the general pattern of the craft guilds.
The university appears to have begun as a scholastic guild.
As craftsmen had done before them, masters and students
banded together for mutual interest and protection and called
themselves a "universitas." "Universitas" was a general
term originally employed to denote any community or corporation, and when used in the modern sense of an educational
body, it required the addition of qualifying words, thus:
Universitas magistrorum et scholarium.[124] In these guilds,
masters and students were related to each other as members
of a guild who had united for the purposes of study: the apprentices were the students; the journeymen, bachelors; the
masters, professors. The guild organization of the university is apparent too in its jurisdiction, its statutes, its de-
pendents and agents whom it possessed in the parchmentmakers and booksellers. The titles of rector, chancellor,
dean, college, and degree are part of guild terminology.[125]

The degree, which originated as a license to teach,
the licentia docendi, admitted its holder to certain honors or
privileges such as those of a craft guild; with it, a professor
might easily move from one university to another. The
chancellor alone bestowed this license to teach. The chancel-

lorship symbolizes the continuity between the cathedral school
and the University of Paris, for even after the university
achieved its own organization, the chancellor of the Chapter
of Notre Dame still reserved the right to grant the licentia
docendi. The chancellor tried to enforce his control of all
education under his jurisdiction, but both teachers and students opposed these attempts. Like other guilds, the universities claimed autonomy, and they did attain a certain amount
of freedom from outside interference. [126] With so large a
student body, much of which was composed of younger students who needed supervision, it is not surprising that the
first guild at Paris was not a guild of students but a guild
of masters. The guild of masters in Paris became the core
of the developing university. [127]

Under the changing conditions which characterized the
early years of development, the difficulties of accommodat-
ing a large influx of predominantly young strangers were
great. The over-exuberance of the students brought about
quarrels among themselves, which often developed into
pitched battles; but if the students contended among themselves, so did the professors in this competitive society.
Both students and masters had disagreements with the civil
authorities. The early history of the university is marked
by open warfare between the opposing factions of "town and
gown." In these early days when the "university" was un-
encumbered with permanent quarters, masters and students
could easily move elsewhere at any time if they felt it necessary to do so. Their most powerful weapon was to strike,
or in medieval terms, to order a "cessation" of lectures.[128]
In the year 1200 certain royal officials had killed some prominent German students in a riot. In protest, all the masters
suspended teaching and threatened to leave Paris. King
Philip II Augustus immediately heeded their demands, punish-
ing the royal officials. [129] Thereafter, the threat of seces-
sion was a powerful weapon. With this power the university
could in one sweeping action suspend all lectures in its halls
and all sermons in the churches of Paris, which would be a
religious deprivation and a civic embarrassment to all citizens. Townsmen feared the loss of prestige won for it by
the university, as well as the loss of revenue which the university afforded. These "cessations" of study sometimes resulted in permanent new foundations. [130] The University of
Oxford apparently arose out of a "migration" of disgruntled
students who, about 1167, left Paris because of quarrels over
the prices of books, clothing, and lodging. A school already
existed at Oxford, but the migration transformed it into a

university. Subsequent cessations at Oxford in 1209 and at
Bologna in 1222 led to the foundation of universities at Cambridge and Padua. [131]

It is with the charter granted in 1200 by Philip Augustus that the University of Paris associates its official foundation, for no university statutes date prior to the thirteenth
century. The charter did not found the university, but recognized it. Toward the end of 1208 Pope Innocent III gave the
masters freedom in the planning of their own regulations. In
1215 the papal legate Robert de Courçon drew up a primitive
body of statutes. Paris had become a university in all but
name. [132]

The outcome of another student riot in 1229, in which
several scholars were slain, was a "great dispersion" of
masters and scholars. Pope Gregory IX induced them to return in 1231 and took the opportunity to make a settlement.
This was the bull Parens Scientarum. [133] This bull has been
called the "Magna Carta" of the University of Paris because
it gave full recognition to the right of the faculties to regu-
late and modify the constitution of the university. [134] The
bull also illustrates one source of academic development,
which was a common desire shared by all kinds of authority
to foster and take pride in the university. The bull is an
expression of favor and protection. Its careful phrases made
it clear that independence implied responsibility and that the
obligation of king, chancellor, citizens, and university alike
was to cooperate with good will in a splendid task, worthy
of the "city of letters, " the "parent of the sciences. " Pope
Gregory went so far as to say that the masters and scholars,
by their departure from Paris, had maintained not so much
their own case as the common cause. The bull was the culminating point in the good relations between the papacy and
the university: the maintenance of their privileges served
the general need of the Church. Later in the thirteenth century Thomas Aquinas was to include among the duties of a
good prince that of promoting centers of learning. [135]

When the informal communities or guilds of teachers
and students thus developed into organized institutions of
learning, they received the corporate stamp that was characteristic of the Middle Ages. The thirteenth-century seal of
the University of Paris illustrates the relationship between
religion and medieval learning. The source of wisdom is
divine, represented at the top by the Virgin and Child,
flanked by Saint Catherine of Alexandria and Saint Nicholas;

at the bottom, two professors are shown teaching. The inscription on the corporate seal of the University of Paris reads, "The seal of the university of masters and scholars at Paris."[136] These were the first real manifestations of the existence of the university. Paris was, therefore, a university city before it had a university.

Other problems affecting the organization of the University of Paris beset the masters during this period of transition. The great diversity of new ideas brought difficulties for the thinkers of the thirteenth century. It was a period of assimilation and the final synthesis of ideas was slow in emerging.[137] The subjects taught in the fully developed universities were many. The new conquests in logic, arithmetic, geometry and astronomy which came with the new learning from the Greek and Arabic translations fell into place without any difficulty in the trivium and the quadrivium framework of the cathedral schools which included the seven liberal arts, to be discussed below, but there was no place for canon or civil law, or for medicine, or for the expansion of theology. A more up-to-date classification of the disciplines and more specialization among teachers was needed.

Masters and students gradually grouped themselves into four faculties: arts, theology, law, and medicine. The faculty of the arts continued the tradition of the trivium and quadrivium. The arts of the trivium included grammar, rhetoric, and logic; and the quadrivium included arithmetic, geometry, astronomy, music, together with scientific, literary, and general culture.[138] The faculty of theology, which was the most famous of the faculties, remained under the control of the Church, and the Church continued to exercise an influence over the supervision of the arts, which varied from time to time according to the institution and the character of particular popes and bishops. The faculty of law, including civil and canonic, and the faculty of medicine were entirely independent of ecclesiastical influence.[139] It is significant to note that there was no faculty of sciences.

Since Paris was the principal school where students went to learn the arts, the faculty of the arts became the largest and most cosmopolitan association of masters. A system of government was gradually devised at the University of Paris which depended upon the organization of the arts faculty. This faculty was divided into four "nations." These nations, which included both professors and scholars, were:

the French, which included Spaniards, Italians, and Greeks; the Picard, representing students from the northeast and the Netherlands; the Norman; and the English, comprising besides students from the provinces under English rule those from England, Ireland, Scotland, and Germany.[140] A dean was elected at the head of each faculty, and the dean of the faculty of the arts was the nominal chief of the university, with the title of rector. He became the executive head of the university by the incorporation under him, first of the students of cannon law and of medicine, which took place about the end of the thirteenth century; and second, of the theologians, which took place about half a century later. The head of each nation had the title of proctor. The only authority remaining to the chancellor of the Cathedral of Notre Dame was the right to accept candidates for degrees recommended by masters of the various faculties. Most of the universities today, whether foreign or American, derive their organization from this academic framework.[141]

Another problem which affected the organization of the University of Paris concerned the mendicant friars. While many of the greatest scholars in the university were to be friars, they nevertheless created an intramural problem. During the years 1252 to 1257 and 1265 to 1271, serious conflict broke out between the secular and the teaching clergy. The friars wished to occupy university chairs and presented for divinity degrees friars who had not followed an arts course. The secular faculty, as anxious to maintain their own interests as to uphold an educational principle, insisted that the arts course was the indispensable preliminary to study in what were recognized as the superior faculties. This conflict was settled by the pope in favor of the mendicants.[142] The Masters' Guild was compelled to recognize the claims of mendicant teachers of theology, although the Masters of Arts managed to exclude them from their faculty; and the friars were to observe the oath of teaching masters and to abide by the university statutes. The quarrel with the mendicants disturbed relations between the university and the papacy, but it also welded the secular faculties more firmly together within the constitutional framework as they rallied against a common danger to their control of the curriculum. This struggle brought about a perfection of the organization of the University of Paris.[143]

As a corporate body, the university was capable of holding property in its own name. As the years went on, the University of Paris built up considerable endowments

through the benefactions of donors. So organized, free from
outside control and enjoying property of its own, the university lived on as an institution beyond the lifetime of all living
men, always to some extent fulfilling its role of conserving
or diffusing knowledge. [144]

These, then, were the essential features of that original institution, the university. The evolution of the guild organization of the University of Paris is itself of interest because it concerns the formal establishment of what has since
been regarded as the best medium for the higher education
of Europe, and because university organization still tends to
reproduce with some modifications the forms first developed
in Paris during the twelfth and thirteenth centuries. The
basic organizational pattern has stood the test of time. The
university, it will be recalled, was not a single school expanding in orderly fashion; it was a confused aggregation of
cosmopolitan students and masters which gradually, through
conflict and adjustment, grew conscious of its unity and extended its privileges. When the nature of the problems which
confronted the University of Paris are considered--the intensity of academic life during its first century of existence,
the ever-increasing number of colleges and halls, the meet-
ings of the nations under their proctors, the various faculties and the competitive nature of academic life, the lectur-
ing and disputations and debates on various subjects, sometimes upon matters affecting the well-being of the Church
itself--the way in which the university maintained its com-
posite unity is proof of the flexibility of its organization and
of its ability to adapt to forces both external and internal as
it passed through the period of formation, growth, and consolidation.

The organization of the University of Paris directly
affected book production. Book production was a factor acting and being acted upon by the forces existent within the society during this period. This subject will be discussed in
depth below. The development of conditions as a result of
controls imposed by the university impeded the growth of the
book production industry before and after the introduction of
printing, and this had adverse effects upon the intellectual
development of the city as well as upon its physical expansion. In the early thirteenth century, however, this period
was still in the future. Far off were the years when Paris
was to suffer disasters not of its making, when the dominant
forces within the social order were to enter upon a period
of strain, when the unique position of Paris in the medieval

world was to become less assured. In the thirteenth century, all the forces active in Paris were in harmonious balance. The city of Paris reached its prime.

Notes

1. Mumford, op. cit., p. 113.

2. Charles T. Wood, The Age of Chivalry (New York: Universe Books, 1970), p. 88.

3. Based upon a concept presented by Mumford, op. cit., p. 562. The application of this concept is the responsibility of the writer.

4. Ibid., p. 96.

5. Ibid., p. 95.

6. Ibid., p. 116.

7. Ibid.

8. Ibid.

9. Ibid., p. 117.

10. Ibid., p. 178.

11. Margaret T. Hodgen, Change and History (Viking Fund Publications in Anthropology No. 18. New York: Wenner-Gren Foundation for Anthropological Research, Inc., 1952), p. 75.

12. Mumford, op. cit., p. 93.

13. Norman F. Cantor, Medieval History (New York: The Macmillan Company, 1963), p. 383.

14. Ibid., p. 589.

15. John Niemeyer Findlay, "Dialectic," Encyclopaedia Britannica (1964 ed.), VII, 356.

16. Cantor, op. cit., p. 397.

17. George Haven Putnam, Books and Their Makers During the Middle Ages (New York: Hillary House Publishers, Ltd., 1962), I, 197-98.

18. Cantor, op. cit., p. 386.

19. Ibid., p. 399.

20. Ibid., p. 403.

21. Ibid., p. 405.

22. Douglas, op. cit., p. 193.

23. Genicot, op. cit., p. 157.

24. Ibid.

25. Cantor, op. cit., pp. 367-68.

26. Ibid., p. 385.

27. Wood, op. cit., p. 94.

28. Ibid., p. 102.

29. Temko, op. cit., p. 188.

30. Wood, op. cit., p. 107.

31. Chester G. Starr and others, A History of the World (Chicago: Rand McNally and Company, 1960), I, 467-68.

32. Wood, op. cit., p. 84.

33. Saalman, op. cit., p. 39.

34. Wood, op. cit., p. 102.

35. Saalman, op. cit., pp. 39-40.

36. Ibid.

37. Henry Adams, Mont-Saint-Michel and Chartres (New York: The Heritage Press, 1933), p. 262.

38. Genicot, op. cit., p. 171.

39. Putnam, op. cit., I, 180-81.

40. Ibid.

41. Richard Hunt, "Universities and Learning, " The Flowering of the Middle Ages, op. cit., p. 197.

42. Ibid.

43. Genicot, op. cit., p. 171.

44. Wood, op. cit., p. 115.

45. Ibid., p. 90.

46. R. W. Southern, The Making of the Middle Ages (New Haven: Yale University Press, 1961), p. 170.

47. Ibid.

48. Ibid., p. 187.

49. Temko, op. cit., p. 69.

50. Emile Mâle, The Gothic Image, trans. Dora Nussey (New York: Harper and Row, 1958), p. vii.

51. Ibid., p. 23.

52. Ibid., p. 390.

53. Ibid., p. 391.

54. Cantor, op. cit., p. 386.

55. Genicot, op. cit., pp. 172-73.

56. Ibid.

57. Douglas, op. cit., p. 189.

58. Lorenzo Minio-Paluello, "Peter Abelard, " Encyclopaedia Britannica (1964 ed.), I, 26.

59. Southern, op. cit., p. 196.

60. Starr and others, op. cit., I, 481.

61. Ibid.

62. Ibid., p. 482.

63. "Universities, " Encyclopaedia Britannica (1964 ed.), XXII, 863.

64. Cantor, op. cit., p. 385.

65. "Universities, " op. cit., p. 864.

66. Adams, op. cit., p. 269.

67. Minio-Paluello, op. cit., p. 26.

68. Ibid.

69. Starr and others, op. cit., I, 483.

70. Genicot, op. cit., p. 158.

71. Cantor, op. cit., p. 397.

72. Laffont, op. cit., p. 29.

73. "Universities, " op. cit., p. 864.

74. Minio-Paluello, op. cit., p. 27.

75. Ibid.

76. Thompson, op. cit., p. 636.

77. Douglas, op. cit., p. 189.

78. Mâle, op. cit., pp. 82-83.

79. Douglas, op. cit., p. 190.

80. James Harvey Robinson, Readings in European History (Boston: Ginn and Company, 1904), p. 447.

81. Ibid.

82. Cantor, op. cit., p. 399.

83. Douglas, op. cit., p. 190.

84. Cantor, op. cit., pp. 399-400.

85. Starr and others, op. cit., I, 483.

86. Carl Stephenson, Mediaeval History (third edition; New York: Harper and Brothers, 1935), p. 263.

87. Ibid.

88. Genicot, op. cit., pp. 157-58.

89. Evans, op. cit., p. 107.

90. "Universities," op. cit., p. 864.

91. Putnam, op. cit., I, 197.

92. Starr and others, op. cit., I, 469.

93. Ibid., p. 492.

94. John B. Morrall, The Medieval Imprint (New York: Basic Books, Inc., 1967), p. 138.

95. R. R. Palmer and Joel Colton, A History of the Modern World (second edition; New York: Alfred A. Knopf, Inc., 1956), p. 38.

96. Genicot, op. cit., p. 157.

97. Putnam, op. cit., I, 198.

98. Minio-Paluello, op. cit., p. 27.

99. Adams, op. cit., p. 280.

100. Joseph Gies and Frances Gies, Life in A Medieval City (New York: Thomas Y. Crowell Company, 1969), p. 154.

101. Robinson, op. cit., p. 453.

102. Adams, op. cit., p. 264.

103. Kurt F. Reinhardt, Germany, 2000 Years (revised

edition; New York: Frederick Ungar Publishing
Company, 1961), p. 138.

104.   Putnam, op. cit., I, 198.

105.   James Westfall Thompson and Edgar Nathaniel John-
       son, An Introduction to Medieval Europe, 300-1500
       (New York: W. W. Norton and Company, Inc.,
       1937), p. 730.

106.   Hunt, op. cit., p. 194.

107.   Putnam, op. cit., I, 221.

108.   Douglas, op. cit., p. 193.

109.   Ibid., p. 181.

110.   Ehrlich, op. cit., p. 133.

111.   Fremantle and others, op. cit., p. 96.

112.   F. M. Powicke, Ways of Medieval Life and Thought
       (Boston: The Beacon Press, 1951), p. 177.

113.   Starr and others, op. cit., I, 488.

114.   Ibid., p. 489.

115.   Hunt, op. cit., p. 194.

116.   "Universities," op. cit., p. 864.

117.   Hunt, op. cit., p. 194.

118.   Ehrlich, op. cit., p. 133.

119.   Douglas, op. cit., p. 189.

120.   Putnam, op. cit., I, 179.

121.   Douglas, op. cit., p. 190.

122.   Putnam, op. cit., I, 179.

123.   Ibid.

124. Genicot, op. cit., p. 187.

125. Georges Renard, Guilds in the Middle Ages (Reprints of Economic Classics. New York: Augustus M. Kelley, 1968), p. 58.

126. Marcel Pierre Pacaut, "Paris University," Encyclopaedia Britannica (1964 ed.), XVII, 304.

127. Douglas, op. cit., p. 190.

128. Hunt, op. cit., p. 193.

129. Stephenson, op. cit., p. 269.

130. Frederick B. Artz, The Mind of the Middle Ages (third edition revised; New York: Alfred A. Knopf, Inc., 1965), pp. 315-16.

131. Hunt, op. cit., p. 193.

132. Pacaut, op. cit., p. 304.

133. Powicke, op. cit., pp. 172-73.

134. "Universities," op. cit., p. 864.

135. Powicke, op. cit., p. 173.

136. Hunt, op. cit., p. 193.

137. Genicot, op. cit., p. 185.

138. Pacaut, op. cit., p. 305.

139. Putnam, op. cit., I, 179.

140. "Universities," op. cit., p. 864.

141. Ibid.

142. Pacaut, op. cit., p. 305.

143. Douglas, op. cit., p. 190.

144. Palmer, op. cit., p. 37.

Chapter 5

MEDIEVAL PARIS: A SYNTHESIS

Thirteenth-century Paris was a capital city: capital
of Europe, capital of Christendom, capital of medieval civilization. With its Capetian monarchy giving secular order to
Europe and furthering the interests of the Heavenly City by
its secular power; with its precious holy relics housed in
the reliquary of glass and stone constructed by a saintly
king; with its cathedral towering above the ramparts identi-
fying the city as an episcopal see; with its university made
famous by the names of Abelard, Lombard, Gratian, Aquinas; with its flourishing mercantile trade capable of supporting a sturdy, industrious bourgeoisie numbering somewhere
around a hundred thousand, the city of Paris could well
claim the status of capital city. When it is recalled, however, that Constantinople in all its sophistication and splendor was the hub of the rich Roman Empire and had been a
city of about a million inhabitants since the time of the
Byzantine emperor Justinian,[1] the status of this first transalpine urban center is placed in proper perspective. Although Paris was a congeries of cities, each little "city"
enriched and supplemented the whole. A summary showing
the synthesis resulting in a state of equilibrium among the
forces of Monarchy, Church, Bourgeoisie and University is
presented here as a description of the daily activities of
Parisians in their medieval setting.

The skyline of thirteenth-century Paris was pierced
by church steeples. The countryside was close at hand.
Fields, orchards, vineyards, and even unused spaces were
spread out at the very gates of the city. Stables, dovecots,
chicken yards filled the city; the air smelled of smoke, hay,
animals. Although Philip Augustus had cobblestoned some
of them, the dark crooked streets became quaggy in wet
weather.[2] Little houses tightly confined within the ramparts
lined the streets, their upper stories cantilevered outward,
their gables jutting on carved wooden beams from which

gargoyles stared, gurgling when slops were tossed down into
the center of the street. The houses jostled shoulder to
shoulder around the cathedral and clustered around the abbeys
and churches. Here and there, architecturally as important
as the churches, were the fine residences of the leading
burgesses and the solid guild halls of drapers, furriers and
others. The crowded bridges were lined with houses. Some
of the buildings which crammed the banks of the river were
suspended over the Seine on stilts.[3] The river, itself as
lively as the streets, was covered with barges, small craft,
ferries, floating timber. Its banks were muddy, furrowed
by carts, tamped down by beasts that came to drink,
trampled by water carriers and stevedores.[4]

        Medieval Paris was a city of charm and respectability,
of energy and vice. The life of the city is reflected in the
panels at the base of the southern transept portal of Notre
Dame Cathedral. Each of these is a picture within a picture,
and between their frames Parisians of 1258 go about their
daily activities. They hurry through streets and squares;
chat, bargain, borrow, greet acquaintances, pass strangers
without recognition. They play with pet dogs, fight with the
gryphons and other mythical beasts of which the minstrels
sang. They accost women, dig deep to find coins for beg-
gars with outstretched hands, take the staff of Saint James
and set off barefooted for Compostela.[5]

        Other sources provide additional glimpses of life in
Paris. In the early decades of the thirteenth century the
right bank, an immense marketplace, was expanding pros-
perously to the wall of Philip Augustus and beyond. Through
narrow streets, pack trains of goods and wagonloads of produce made their way among a walking populace of merchants,
artisans, laborers, serfs, priests, begging friars, stout
bourgeois housewives; they left as laden as they had entered.
Between the Templars' temple and the Louvre, streets were
lined with bakeries, spice shops, meat shops famous for
their hams; with elegant shops of merchants, craftsmen's
workshops, cheap bazaars, produce stalls.[6] The squares
were loud with the cries of fishmongers, vegetable hawkers,
town criers; with the sound of church bells.[7] Through the
gate toward the faubourg Saint Denis and the international
fairground, the Lendit Fair was held each June, specializing
in the requirements of the university, for which it had no
equal. The solemn procession of the university to the Lendit, stretching over miles of street and lane, was magnificent.[8]

Spilling over to the left bank is the Latin Quarter.
Here, where wolves had still appeared in the winter in Abelard's time, colleges which donors were beginning to establish wedged themselves among the mendicant foundations on
the slopes. The left bank and the Cité were crowded with
students, thinkers, artisans, craftsmen, traders. Scholars
were discovering the intellectual tracks of Abelard and his
followers all around them and were experiencing that rare
satisfaction which comes with the sense of being privileged
to study in the vital center of a new cultural era, and they
found it intoxicating.[9] This Latin Quarter roared with argu-
mentative life. Students thronged the schools and crowded
the cafes and chattered their Latin. They argued, shouted,
sang, drank, picnicked, gambled, fought. They played wild
pranks on the bourgeoisie and escaped from the exasperated
police, while their masters secured papal and royal recognition and a seal for the university. In the twelfth century
Saint Bernard had called this academic city a Babylon, inviting the students to join him in the solitude of Clairvaux,
with not much success.[10] Well-to-do students enjoyed the
luxury of possessing books, while the not-so-fortunate could
be seen laboriously transporting huge and heavy leather
volumes or parchments back and forth between lodgings and
classrooms.[11] Here and there among the students and professors, stationarii, scribes, and copyists, who had quickly
gathered and attached themselves to the university, went
about their business; and booksellers bargained and bartered
in their booths along the quays and bridges and churches.

At the center of all, uniting right bank and left bank,
drawing all of Paris and all of France together was the Ile
de la Cité, the seat of the Crown. The island was separated
between the Church and the Crown by the central commercial
street that ran from bridge to bridge. The eastern end of
the island was dominated by the cathedral, and the western
end by the palace of the Capets, located on the site of the
present Palais de Justice. Philip Augustus lived here in the
palace of his fathers when he was not fighting and camped in
the field, or hunting, or enjoying the hospitality of his vassals. Here he dispensed justice, levied taxes, formulated
strategy, presided over the royal court.[12] Throughout the
thirteenth century important feudatories would kneel in the
Capetian throne room, place their hands between those of the
king, and surrender privileges, wealth, and eventually their
independence to Philip and his sons.[13] In the full Capetian
power of the thirteenth century, Saint Louis lived by prefer-
ence in the palace; and he built his Sainte-Chapelle in its

court. Under the Capets, the Louvre remained what Philip
Augustus had planned it to be: the key outer defense of
Paris.[14]

   The episcopal community, a city within a city, surrounded Notre Dame Cathedral. Around this cathedral crowds
moved beneath the sculptures; pilgrims knelt before the sta-
tues, bathed in the warm, many-colored light filtering through
the transept roses. Processions wound out of the aisles,
leaving the cathedral by the southern transept and making a
circuit of the nave, the cross held before the multitude, and
returning through the northern transept to the altar. To the
south of the cathedral, the bishop's palace was a center of
activity. Sergeants lounged in its hallways and guarded its
gates. Lawyers argued cases at the bishop's court of justice; in the exchequer, bailiffs reported the collection of
tithes, tolls, taxes; clerks settled accounts and stacked
coins on the ruled table; archivists entered all these transactions into the records.[15] Outside the office of the chancellor, students waited to inquire after their bourses or to
answer for breaches in discipline, passing the time by shoot-
ing dice on the bishop's stairway. In the bishop's courtyard powerful guilds of masters, journeymen, apprentices,
accompanied by their wives, marched in ranks regularly
year after year across the parvis, carrying banners and
singing, to make gifts to Notre Dame. These guilds endowed
chapels, windows, statuary, altar vessels, ornaments of
every kind, competing with each other in their generosity to
the cathedral. Ordinary people, who were necessary to this
episcopal community and always welcome, enrolled their sons
in church, registered deeds, paid taxes, asked for welfare,
stood before the law. Sometimes they just came to watch
the arrivals and departures of the great: the king or bishop
or archdeacons of Notre Dame galloping with companies of
horsemen through the cobbled courtyard between the palace
and the cathedral; or barons with troops of knights.[16]
Sometimes they just came to enjoy freely, here in the house
they shared with God, the candles, silver, gold, tapestries,
carvings, paintings, stained glass windows; the smell of
incense; the choral harmonies of hyms and chants; reveling
in the luxury of space and light and sound: all the richness
denied them elsewhere in their world. Here in the Heavenly
City, worshippers standing in their thousands--king, baron,
noble; knight, sergeant, serf; bishop, archbishop, priest,
friar, pilgrim; professor, student, bookseller, stationarius,
scribe; burgess, artisan, craftsman; merchant, trader, fish-
monger--each experienced a momentary insight into the in-

describable glories of heavenly life. Outside on the western
façade standing poised high above the city on the balustrade
before the rose window, the Virgin flanked by angels points
out the activities of her city to the Child cradled against her
shoulder.

        Medieval Paris was a vibrant, cosmopolitan city, a
microcosm of Western Christendom, reflecting all that was
best and most characteristic in the culture of the age. It
was also intensely individual. "A capital city, " wrote Traill,
"whatever else it may or may not be, is almost always
characteristic. It is what it is because its people are what
they are. "[17] Medieval Paris represented Europe by being
itself, and it bequeathed to the future its own intense personality. "To be French, to be a Parisian, " wrote Ehrlich,
"is to be the sum of the national experience. "[18]

Function of the City

        Mercantile city, royal city, ecclesiastical city, uni-
versity city: each grew out of a unique situation; each presented a unique constellation of forces; each translated into
physical structures its own unique solution. Church, Monarchy, University: these, according to a medieval writer,
were the three powers which guarded the health of Christendom.[19] During its long history, first one force then another
monopolized the creative powers of the city of Paris, and
the dominant structures of the city expressed that monopoly.
These forces served as formative elements of medieval
Paris,[20] shaping every quarter of the city. The immediate
topographical and geographical characteristics of the city's
surroundings, as has been noted, exercised an influence on
the early development so that the organic division of "town,
city, and university of Paris" corresponds to the natural
division of the site. These three forces, combined with the
fourth, the Bourgeoisie, who provisioned the city, converged
upon the city of Paris in the thirteenth century. As the
growing capital of the Capetian kingdom and located at the
crossroads of medieval Europe, Paris was the ideal place
for the pieces to be put together and welded into a whole.

        The close harmony which prevailed among these forces
was the primary factor in promoting the greatness of Paris
during its Golden Age. It was a harmony resulting from the
balance of positives and negatives in fine adjustment, an equilibrium in which the negative forces were latent. Although

Philip Augustus constructed his fortress of the Louvre outside the city walls in order to be able if necessary to defend the city, he never had to use the stronghold for this purpose. Although the Church impregnated every Parisian activity at this time, fostering the guilds, inspiring the scholarship and art of the city, giving special sanction to the monarchy, both Church and monarchy were consistently friendly to the rising university without over-regulating its activities. All the activities of the city were united in relation to a common purpose. There was to be much notable achievement in Paris in later times, but it was not again to be accompanied by such confident equilibrium.[21] Paris was the focal point dominant enough to assimilate and to transmute what it received, and the city contained within itself all the elements of a great expansion.[22] Only through the harmonious combination of these essential characteristics was Paris enabled to discharge its special function in the history of Europe and to perform its cultural role as a university city.

Mumford believed that perhaps the three most essential functions of the city are cultural storage, dissemination and interchange, and creative addition.[23] Society is accumulative, and the city became the essential organ of that process. The city from its origin onward, Mumford stated, may be described as a structure especially equipped to store and to transmit the cultural heritage. The invention of forms such as the handwritten manuscript, the archive, the library, the university, is one of the most characteristic achievements of the city.[24] The development of symbolic methods of storage increased the capacity of the city to hold together a larger body of people and institutions than any other kind of community and to maintain and transmit a larger portion of their lives than individual human memories could transmit by word of mouth. Storage for the purpose of enlarging the boundaries of the community in time and space, Mumford pointed out elsewhere, is one of the important functions performed by the city, and the degree to which it is performed partly establishes the rank and value of the city.[25]

The city's three functions of cultural storage, dissemination and interchange, and creative addition, were adequately performed in the University of Paris. The university also made explicit in its own right as a secular function another of the necessary activities of the city: the withdrawal from immediate practical responsibilities and the critical reappraisal and renewal of the cultural heritage through the direct intercourse of master and student.[26] Like the city to which it owed its birth, the University of Paris in the thirteenth century, Christian in its scholarship, universal in its interests and membership, reflected all that was best and most characteristic in the culture of the age.

Notes

1. Starr and others, op. cit., I, 244.

2. Zoe Oldenbourg, "With Stone and Faith," The Horizon Book of Great Cathedrals, Jay Jacobs, editor (New York: American Heritage Publishing Company, Inc., 1968), p. 22.

3. Temko, op. cit., pp. 164-65.

4. Oldenbourg, op. cit., p. 23.

5. Temko, op. cit., p. 258.

6. Ibid., p. 164.

7. Ibid., p. 70.

8. Ibid., p. 164.

9. Cantor, op. cit., pp. 383-84.

10. Temko, op. cit., p. 67.

11. Thompson, op. cit., p. 638.

12. Temko, op. cit., p. 70.

13. Ibid., p. 164.

14. Ibid., p. 70.

15. Ibid., pp. 253-54.

16. Ibid.

17. H. D. Traill (ed.), "Introduction," The Capitals of the World (New York: Harper and Brothers, 1894), p. xiii.

18. Ehrlich, op. cit., p. 108.

19. Douglas, op. cit., p. 193.

20. Ibid.

21. Ibid.

22. Genicot, op. cit., p. 236.

23. Mumford, op. cit., p. 276.

24. Ibid., pp. 30-31.

25. Ibid., p. 98.

26. Ibid., p. 276.

Chapter 6

TEACHING METHODS

Like the cathedral, the university is a product of the Middle Ages. The university was the one institution outside the Church which survived from the old guilds, perhaps the most important single new institution produced by the medieval culture.[1] Although the University of Paris arose from the cooperation of the two chief forces of Church and Monarchy, it always possessed its own inherent life. Organized as a special guild whose purpose was to educate men, the guild through its masters set the length and time a student had to serve as an apprentice and a journeyman, established the conditions under which he could enter into the ranks of the masters, and regulated the conditions under which its members performed their work, the final requirement for receiving the degree being a comprehensive oral examination. The degree, technically a license to teach, was a certificate of competence in the craft pursued by the guild corporation. The corporate character of this guild of masters was more formally recognized when it was allowed to plead by means of a proctor, to elect common officers, and to use a common seal.[2]

The significance of the corporate character of its guild or organization is that it assured to the University of Paris as a learned corporation, and to other universities which followed this same pattern, the right to independence and a separate existence with its own regulations as to membership and duties. It gave a collective organization to those who had a license and made teaching their profession, and to those who, wherever they came from and whatever their personal status, desired instruction leading to an academic degree within a framework which insured continuity. This organization provided the free interchange of thought among independent and qualified professors.[3] It meant that the pursuit of knowledge did not depend for its existence or continuance upon any specific texts or curricula. The independence of the university from the standards of the market and the city, Mumford pointed out, fostered the special sort of authority it exercised: the sanction of verifiable truth ratified by the methods of logic and dialectic, authoritative scholarship, and scientific method, as these in turn have developed and accumulated from period to period.[4] As the Church ceased to be the repository of new values, the university gradually took over some of this function. The freedom from episcopal jurisdiction, which made the university directly answerable to Rome, widened the scope of the curriculum, but it also allowed a greater control by the pope of its orthodoxy, which was further increased by the entry of the mendicant orders. It was in having this corporate identity that medieval universities resembled those of today and differed from the schools of Athens or Alexandria in ancient times.[5]

Retaining the old, reaching for the new: this was the character of the city of Paris as the microcosm of Western civilization. Indications of this blend of old and new were also apparent in the development of the curriculum of the cathedral school into that of the University of Paris, and in the manner in which these subjects were taught. The main thrust of the following discussion is the scientific method. It is prefaced by a definition of terms, by a general survey of the traditional method of teaching showing the continuity of the educational tradition from classical times, and by Capella's personification of the seven liberal arts of the trivium and quadrivium which permeated medieval culture. The discussion is limited to those aspects of the subject which pertain to book production and is intended to be descriptive rather than analytical.

"Teaching," for the purposes of this study, is defined as the stimulation of learning; and "learning," the active process carried on through doing, reacting, undergoing. "Methods of teaching" is understood to include those things that are done to stimulate learning, and these methods must necessarily take into account the nature of learning and of the learner. "Method" is considered to be any organized, systematic procedure through which any activities that go beyond the routine are carried on. "Techniques" and "devices" are parts within a method.[6]

Traditional Method

The great masters in the University of Paris during
its developmental period were not only notable scholars
themselves, they were also great teachers developing the
older educational system of the trivium and quadrivium of
the cathedral schools into one which, as Douglas expressed
it, might stand comparison with that of any age.[7] The
framework of the studies in the cathedral schools was designed to communicate instruction in the seven liberal arts,
a cycle canonized in the Carolingian age, which constituted
the educational curriculum of the Middle Ages. The curriculum of these earlier schools had been inherited from Rome
through Martianus Capella (fl. late fourth and early fifth century A.D.) and Boethius (470?-525).[8] Capella distinguished
seven liberal arts. Boethius later divided these into the
trivium of grammar, rhetoric, and logic, and the quadrivium
comprising arithmetic, geometry, music, and astronomy.
About the same time as Boethius was transmitting some
meager fragments of Greek learning to the world of the
Middle Ages, Cassiodorus produced his De artibus ac disci-
plinis liberalium litterarum, a complete manual of the liberal arts for his monks at Vivarium, to whom he tried to
demonstrate that the seven liberal arts were indispensable
to the understanding of the Scriptures.[9] The seven liberal
arts of the trivium and the quadrivium opened out to medieval man seven paths of human activity by which he advanced
from manual labor to instruction. The sequence of the
labors of the twelve months accompanied by the signs of the
zodiac were carved in stone on the façades of cathedrals; in
Paris, they appeared on the west façade of Notre Dame. In
these labors of the months, the laborer recognized the un-
ceasing round of work to which all his life long he was destined, but the Virgin looking down upon these earthly things
reminded him that he did not labor without hope.[10]

The Middle Ages could not conceive the seven liberal
arts other than in the guise of seven majestic maidens, and
this personification appeared for the first time in the famous
treatise of the fifth-century African rhetorician Martianus
Capella entitled The Marriage of Philology and Mercury.[11]
In this work Capella created types, and the types created
engraved themselves more deeply on the memory of the
Middle Ages than did the subsequent creations of the great
masters. From the time of Gregory of Tours in the late
sixth century, some knowledge of Capella's book was believed to be indispensable for every clerk. From that time

onward, the poets could not forget the descriptions of Capella
when they personified the seven liberal arts in verse. [12] In
the eleventh, twelfth, and thirteenth centuries, the records
show that Capella's book had a place in the collections of
most monasteries and cathedrals. The types created by
Capella were generally accepted by thirteenth-century writers
as well as by artisans and craftsmen, and are represented
visually in the sculpture of the cathedrals. [13] The earliest
representations of the arts are found on the façades of Laon
and Chartres. On entering Chartres through the Royal Portal, the worshiper was reminded by the personification of the
seven liberal arts that faith needed to be enlightened by reason and knowledge. [14] Until the Renaissance, definite traces
of their influences are seen in art, in sculpture, in stained
glass windows, in tapestries, and in handwritten manuscripts.
Since the seven liberal arts formed the basis of the curriculum of the Cathedral School of Notre Dame out of which the
University of Paris grew, it is believed useful to present a
brief description of these types as Capella described them, [15]
and as cited by Mâle.

Capella believed that the graces of the imagination
would ease the severity of learning, and so he opened his
manual with a romance. The god Mercury asks for the
hand of Philology in marriage and presents himself on the
wedding day with a retinue of the seven arts. Each para-
nymph--in Ancient Greece, the friends who went with the
bridegroom in a chariot to fetch home the bride--comes
forward in turn, giving a long discourse in the presence of
the god, which is a complete treatise on the art she represents. Grammar, the first of the seven, comes forward
dressed in a long sleeveless Roman cloak, holding an ivory
case resembling a doctor's instrument case, implying that
grammar is the true therapeutic which cures all defects of
speech. In her case, among other things, may be seen ink,
pens, candlesticks, tablets, a file in eight sections marked
by gold lines symbolizing the eight parts of speech, and a
scalpel with which she operates on the tongue and teeth to
facilitate utterance. Rhetoric is an armed maiden, beautiful, tall, graceful, a helmet covering her hair, who comes
forward to the sound of trumpets brandishing formidable
weapons. Precious stones glitter on her breast, and count-
less figures are embroidered upon her cloak. Dialectic fol-
lows, a thin woman draped in a black mantle with bright
eyes shining in a pale face, her hair dressed in elaborate
rolls. In her left hand she holds a serpent half hidden under
her robe; in the right, a wax tablet and a fishhook. The

attributes of Dialectic were explained in a commentary written in the tenth century by Remigius of Auxerre. According
to this commentary, Mâle explained, the rolled hair denotes
the syllogism; the serpent, the wiles of sophistry; and the
hook stands for insidious argument.16   The robe which Geometry wears is also embroidered with figures. These figures show the movements of the stars, the shadow that the
earth casts upon the sky, and the signs of the gnomon. The
gnomon, a notched instrument, the position or length of
whose shadow served as an indicator of the hour of the day,
was a precursor of the sundial. In her right hand Geometry
holds a pair of compasses; in her left, a globe; and before
her is a table thick with greenish dust in which she draws
her figures. Arithmetic has the stately beauty of a primitive goddess. From her forehead issues a ray which, dividing, becomes double, then triple, then quadruple; after
multiplying itself to infinity, it again becomes one. Her
fingers move with incredible rapidity, symbolizing, explained
the commentary of Remigius, the rapidity of her calculations.
Astronomy bursts forth from an aureole of flame, a crown
of stars on her glittering hair. She spreads a pair of golden
wings with crystal feathers and carries a bent and gleaming
instrument for observing stars. The book composed of
various metals which she holds, commented Remigius, represents the various zones which she studies. The last of the
maidens is Music, the beautiful Harmonia, who comes forward with a train of goddesses, poets and musicians.
Around her Orpheus, Arion, Amphion, Pleasure, and Grace
all sing sweetly while she draws indescribably beautiful
strains from a large shield of gold strung with resounding
strings. She is pure harmony, and at each movement the
little golden discs on her dress tinkle melodiously.17   Medieval man was dazzled by the figures of these radiant women.

No prominent representation of the seven liberal arts
was to be found at Notre Dame Cathedral where the "university" was rapidly developing in Paris, the town called by
Gregory IX "the town of books, " although Mâle believes that
the trumeau or pillar which supported the statue of Christ
in the central doorway was at one time decorated with the
figures of the arts. While the liberal arts were not visually
represented on the façade of Notre Dame, the curriculum
of its cathedral school was based upon them, and the curriculum of the University of Paris was erected upon this framework. The trivium and quadrivium remained the standard
classification of the liberal arts throughout the scholastic
period.18

no discussion in these early years. The only Socratic dialogue was among the masters themselves, and they engaged
in great public debates on disputed theses. Examinations
were conducted in the form of the "disputation, " a verbal en-
counter in which an opinion was attacked and defended according to rules of dialectical argument. Until about 1125, teaching and research were thus a matter of commentary on the
classical authorities. [27]

All the lectures as well as the commentaries based
upon them were in Latin, the universal language of the
Middle Ages. Latin was used in the schools, in the church,
and in public administration. The use of Latin meant that
ideas could have a wide currency across all frontiers. [28]

Manuscripts, being handwritten on expensive parchment, were too costly to be possessed by ordinary students.
Those who could afford them watched them carefully. Others
clubbed together to buy them, and at Paris many volumes
were rented to students long before the establishment of
libraries. [29] For the student without a text it was important
to take notes. Since paper was not yet in use, and since
the expense of using parchment was prohibitive, students
took notes on wax tablets using a stylus of bone, ivory, or
metal. The whitish scratches it made on the black or green
wax could be erased by rubbing with its rounded end. Students used wax tablets to the beginning of the fifteenth century. Students might also pool their resources to buy parchment; then after the lecture was over they could record what
they remembered of the lecture. The resulting notebook became common property and was passed from hand to hand
for study. [30]

An essential feature of the oral lecture was the training of memory. Without notes, the student could only rely
on memory to retain what he heard. Memory and oral exer-
cises were therefore indispensable. [31]

Education by the twelfth century was entirely dependent upon the text as presented by the "authorities"; that is,
the ancients and the Church Fathers, a fact which had far-
reaching implications for both book production and for development of the scientific method. The work of instruction
rested directly upon mastery of the text itself. A subject
was taught not directly and in itself, but by the explanation
of books which derived their authority solely from their
writers. "Taking a course" in a subject meant actually

reading a book on that subject. Learning thus was circumscribed by the limitations of the master and the boundaries
of available knowledge. [32]

While instruction was dependent upon the use of books,
at the same time the nature of the instruction did not call
for a large supply of books; that is, the master could own
those which he himself needed for his teaching and if others
were needed he might borrow them. The twelfth-century
curriculum reveals the paucity of material available for the
study of the liberal arts. Logic alone could be studied
seriously in depth. [33]

Not all monastic and cathedral schools, however, offered a full curriculum in the liberal arts; many had to re-
strict themselves to the mere rudiments of education, while
others placed heavier emphasis upon a curriculum more
suitable for the training of monks and priests. In the north
the cathedral schools were essentially schools of the arts,
and in Paris of logic in particular. [34] When the new learning invaded the cathedral schools in the twelfth century, only
a very few of them developed into universities. These universities took the lead in higher education, and the grammar
schools of the towns and guilds became centers of elementary education, while those cathedral schools which remained
continued, as noted, to instruct most of the candidates for
the priesthood. [35]

With the twelfth century a new epoch began. In the
first place, the methods of dialectic, no longer studied as a
discipline in schools, begin to be applied to problems of
theology; in the second place, the whole of Aristotle's
Organon became known to Western Europe about 1130 and
began to be studied there; and finally, the University of
Paris came into existence as an organized body and provided the framework in which the whole of Aristotelian writings might find a place. [36]

With regard to the first factor, two great influences
shaped medieval thought: the tradition of ancient logic and
the system of Christian theology. The correlative development of logic in the twelfth century led to another step for-
ward--a belief in reason, and particularly reason as the
chief instrument of scholarship. As early as the eleventh
century, Berengar of Tours had argued that "true courage
lies in flying to dialectic in all things, since to fly to it is
to fly to reason." [37] Anselm of Canterbury deemed reason

capable of confirming and renewing the truths of revelation.
Bonizo of Sutri, Irnerius, and Abelard required that it should
reconcile and unify the branches of knowledge. To Bernard
of Clairvaux and many other churchmen, however, the application of dialectic to the things of faith appeared as dangerous as it was impious. To the end of the medieval period
philosophy centers upon the discussion of the same problems
of logic which began to agitate the teachers of the earlier
centuries.[38] Dialectic, it may be noted, is to begin with a
merely secular art and only by degrees were its terms and
distinctions applied to the subject matter of theology.

The second factor for change relates to the arrival
of Greek and Arabic learning. The study of Boethius's
treatises and the logic of Aristotle dominated the early
Middle Ages. Down to the beginning of the twelfth century
only the earlier and more elementary parts of his Organon
were known and studied. Although it was only a small fragment of Aristotle, this first half was, nevertheless, enough
to provoke thought and to give men a familiarity with the
method and outline of Aristotle's logic. It was a considerable instrument of education for many centuries, forming the
basis of dialectic. As such, Aristotle was the chief influence, excluding theology, in the educational system of the
early Middle Ages.[39]

Aristotle was the inventor of the syllogism, and he
invented the science of logic.[40] While there was reasoning
before Aristotle, Aristotle was the first to make its methods
and rules explicit. His Organon sets forth the system of
deductive thinking and learning. In the deductive method of
teaching the basic principle, generalization or law is set
down first, together with illustrations. The student is led
to analyze the principle and examples and then to find new
ones in the field of study.[41]

Of the treatises of the Organon, Abelard knew only
the first two, the De interpretatione and the Categories, the
first treating of the constituent parts and kinds of sentences,
and the second of the classes of logical propositions. With
Abelard the fusion of the reasoning methods of dialectic with
theology was more complete than that of previous masters.
He sought to rationalize in categories of formal logic every
matter apprehended by his mind.[42] Abelard's purpose was
not to destroy faith by a mere exposure of inconsistencies,
but to point beyond the inconsistencies of tradition to a recon-
ciliation. His conceptualism combined the analytic and the

synthetic points of view.   It is notable in two ways: it ap-
proximated to the doctrine of Aristotle in the Posterior Ana-
lytics, which were not known in Paris until twenty years
after Abelard's death; and it emphasized the creative power
of reason.   The reasoning mind, Abelard believed, arrives
at universals, and thus constitutes the universe of thought.43
Abelard believed that reason and intelligence must do the
preparatory work of solving or reconciling inconsistencies before faith can have a consistent body of belief which alone
is credible.   In this way reason became the basis of a new
intellectual technique.   The teacher no longer merely glossed
the authorities, explaining the texts line by line.   He quoted
all the authorities on the question, and alone or in discussion
with his student, he would attempt to arrive at a synthesis
by the operation of reason. 44

        The technique of teaching used by the masters of
Paris in addition to lectures was the "disputation, " in which
two or more masters and occasionally the students debated
text readings employing Abelard's question-and-answer approach. 45   This exercise in various forms soon came to
dominate academic life.   The subjects for disputation,
whether in grammar, logic, or theology, arose out of questions raised in the lectures or textbooks.   By the last quarter of the twelfth century the discussion of "questions" had
become an independent exercise.   Careful rules were later
formulated.   The disputation became the academic exercise
par excellence: "determining" a question was the act by
which a bachelor became a master. 46

        Dialectic, the technique of reasoning by dialogue as
a method of intellectual investigation, was differently interpreted at different times.   In the early period, it consisted
of the barest essentials of elementary, formal logic, a
course usually offered to beginners.   Aristotle's universe,
however, is dynamic, and this kind of material in the hands
of a dynamic personality such as Abelard was destined to
exercise a profound influence on the trend of culture.   Dialectic became a sport and a passion.   A student would pass
rapidly through grammar and rhetoric to arrive at the excitements of logic. 47   There was a concentration on logic
which underlay all higher education, and it attained great
prestige.   When Henry I was entertaining Pope Callixtus II
in 1119, the high point of the entertainment was a disputation by two young nobles, the sons of the Count of Moulan.
As a form of entertainment it outlasted the Middle Ages.
As late as the sixteenth century when Queen Elizabeth I

visited Oxford, the university arranged for the performance of a disputation. [48] The position of dialectic throughout the thirteenth century is reflected in the Summulae of Petrus Hispanus (d. 1277), which long continued to be the most widely read textbook of logic. Regarding dialectic, Hispanus wrote:

> Dialectic is the art of arts, the science of sciences, furnishing the way to the principles of all methods. For dialectic alone discusses accurately the principles of all other sciences and therefore in the attainment of sciences dialectic should be the first.[49]

Guérard believes it was perhaps at this time that the French acquired the taste for protracted and animated logical discussion, which is still one of their characteristics. [50]

The technique of disputation spread into written works, and in the latter part of the thirteenth century came to dominate exposition. The Summa Theologiae of Thomas Aquinas, for example, is built up out of a series of articles in each of which the arguments for and against are presented in the form of syllogisms. The reply, which forms the body of the article, is then given; finally, any difficulties remaining in the arguments against are disposed of. [51]

Although its application to the problem of theology gave rise to much soul-searching, logic seemed to be the key to the understanding of all problems. The tradition of relying on logic rather than entirely on faith and authority culminated in Scholasticism. Abelard's approach formulated the methodology of Scholasticism. The discovery of the laws of the syllogism, of logical demonstration, and of the refutation of false conclusions enlarged the intellectual horizon. The student learned to classify the types of valid argument, to detect the causes of error, and to unmask the process of deception. [52] Scholasticism, the process of painstaking arrival at logical conclusions through questioning, postulating, examining, and arranging details into a system of logic, developed within this context. [53]

The followers of Abelard used the method which he had first developed in rudimentary form, multiplying the questions, following the questions with logical arguments pro and con, citing previously held views by learned churchmen, and terminating with the logical conclusion. Thus the dialectical method involves a triadic process, consisting of a prefatory statement of the arguments and counterarguments of a given proposition, followed by the solution of the problem, and finally, the answering point by point of the initial objections on the basis of the solution contained in the main part of the article.[54] The method of Abelard was thus perfected by his followers, who went one step further than Abelard: they provided a solution.

While the scholars of the thirteenth century recovered the ancient principles of logical reasoning, they also discovered fresh material on which to exercise them. Contact with the East by trade and in the Crusades and with the Moors in Spain had further stimulated intellectual life. By the time that Abelard's disciple Peter Lombard was completing his Sentences, new knowledge poured into Europe, bringing about an intellectual revolution. The more advanced logical essays of Aristotle had appeared in Latin, to take their place as the new logic in the prescribed dialectic of the schools. By the end of the twelfth century, Western scholars were also supplied with Latin versions of Ptolemy, Galen, Hippocrates and other Greek authors, as well as scores of books by Avicenna and other Arabs. The philosophical and scientific writings of Aristotle were for the most part translated early in the thirteenth century, together with a mass of Arabic commentary, particularly that of Averroës.[55] The assimilation of Aristotle's logic was the intellectual task which absorbed the energy of the greatest minds of the period from the end of the tenth to the end of the twelfth century. Under the influence of this assimilation, the method of theological speculation underwent a profound change. The change was felt most keenly in the field of theology, although every department of thought was similarly affected. The methods of logical arrangement and analysis and, more importantly, the habits of thought associated with the study of logic penetrated the studies of law, politics, grammar, rhetoric, to mention but a few.[56] The Aristotle now transmitted to Western Europe was strongly influenced by the philosophical and theological convictions of the Arabic translations and commentaries and had to be reinterpreted in terms of Christianity. It was the Dominican scholar Thomas Aquinas who accomplished the great synthesis of Platonic, Aristotelian, and Christian philosophy. Philosophy and theology were harmonized in the dialectical processes of the Aristotelian syllogism.[57] No sooner was the harmony apparently established, however, than Duns Scotus began his negative criticism, which was carried much further by William of Occam. In Nominalism, to be discussed below, the enemies of Saint Thomas Aquinas were to triumph.

Another type of material which became available for study and disputation, eventually finding a place in the curriculum of Western European studies, was the "summa." The standard commentary or "gloss" was, as noted, the work of the twelfth-century masters. These same masters began to make collections of these glosses or "sentences, " as they came to be called, on the chief topics of theology; and these would comprise the summa. The summa summed up the learning of the past in many fields of study, Peter Lombard's Sentences (c1150) superseding all earlier collections. [58] The summa was an instrument for the advancement of knowledge; from the beginning it was alive with discussion. Quite early in the twelfth century a demand grew for a reliable version of the master's lecture. A number of these summae appeared throughout the twelfth and thirteenth centuries, and these works, along with those of the ancients, found a place as textbooks in the curricula of medieval universities. With the summa, the thinker freed himself from the literal commentary. Exegesis was no longer enough. The scholar began to argue from the particular to the general, to induce from the application the principle which justified it and thus bring everything into a system. [59]

The two factors discussed thus far which ushered in the new epoch with the twelfth century were the application of the dialectical method to problems of theology and the introduction of the whole of Aristotle's Organon into Western Europe, which had brought about the concentration upon logic, the development of dialectic, and the growth of Scholasticism. The third new factor was the coming into existence of the University of Paris, which provided the academic framework in which the whole of Aristotelian writings might find a place.

With the renewed intellectual vitality of the later Middle Ages, the intense theological debates and the founding of Scholasticism were to place Aristotelian thought and method in a dominant position. In the Christian world, Scholasticism became the dominant mode of thought. The widespread intellectual ferment, the zeal in disputation characteristic of Scholasticism, and the growth of cities all contributed to the creation and development of universities. The universities of the time based their courses heavily on Aristotle and aided in the production of the great scholastics, Peter Lombard, Alexander of Hales, Albert Magnus, Thomas Aquinas.[60] The effect of the new knowledge upon the curriculum of the University of Paris was slow. The earliest university statutes at Paris in 1215 present only a sketchy outline of a curriculum. They imply lectures in arts and theology. Ethics is an optional subject, while the two Aristotelian "philosophies," with the writings of certain heretics, are prohibited studies. By 1255 lectures are prescribed on the Metaphysics, Physics, De anima, De caelo et mundo of Aristotle and a range of books on natural philosophy.[61] The entry of the mendicant orders on the left bank in the early thirteenth century brought about a great change in the higher studies, after much conflict, which increased the emphasis upon theology. This shift in emphasis created problems of censorship and regulation which had a reflex action upon book production. By 1323 the Paris university was the most important in Europe for theological studies,[62] and the Latin Quarter became an ecclesiastical commonwealth independent of the king.[63] In 1452 a drastic reform was effected at Paris and the full arts course included grammar in more modern textbooks, verse-making, logic, algorism, geometry, and astronomy, and subsequent to the bachelor's degree, mathematics, which included arithmetic, geometry, music, and Aristotle's three "philosophies."[64] As early as 1458, the teaching of Greek was permitted at the conservative University of Paris, by now the headquarters of scholastical philosophical theology.[65] Throughout the Middle Ages the learning of France was an integral part of the learning of Europe, and Paris became the intellectual center of Christendom, which served to raise French learning above the limits of nationality. National distinctions of scholars were meaningless, for all scholars were citizens of the Christian commonwealth, the intellectual capital of which was the University of Paris.[66] In the not too distant future, however, education at the University of Paris was to become enmeshed in the complex religious struggle that shattered the unity of Christendom.

The Aristotelian revelation and the rapid growth of the University of Paris contributed to bringing about the golden age of Scholasticism. Taken in its widest sense, Scholasticism was merely the system of education that characterized the early universities, a system that bore the unmistakable marks of Abelard's influence.[67] With Abelard, dialectic in the twelfth century had come to dominate intellectual life. In the thirteenth century, medieval thought became academic or "scholastic." All the important writers on theology, philosophy, law, and science were "scholastics"; that is, they were professors in the schools and universities who were devoted to the use of the dialectical method of reason-

ing and exposition. [68] During the later thirteenth and early
fourteenth centuries, scholastic learning provided a sound
education in the universities. Scholasticism was the medieval system of education to prepare men in the arts and professional subjects. It included such fields as mathematics,
science, philosophy, logic, theology, and Roman and canon
law. This education was a tremendous improvement over
any since the Roman Empire. [69] By the fourteenth century,
interest in dialectic had begun to decline. The method had
developed in some sense at the expense of content. Evans
provides a quotation from Robert de Sorbon which illustrates
the typical attitude:

> Does not he who day and night practices the tor-
> tures of dialectic walk in the way of vanity and dark-
> ness of the mind? Is not the laborer mad who is
> for ever sharpening his ploughshare without ever
> ploughing the field? The art of dialectic should
> sharpen the mind, but in order to prepare it for
> greater things. [70]

The serious weaknesses of Scholasticism were lack of emphasis on literature, ignorance of knowledge developing outside the university, and failure to appreciate adequately the
empirical method, thus forfeiting knowledge provided by experience. [71] By the fifteenth century, Scholasticism connoted
a system of learning devoted to argumentation over subjects
of no importance. At its best, on the other hand, it forced
the individual to analyze intellectual problems and to use his
reason. The technique of disputation, which was the essence
of medieval teaching, had required both master and student
to argue and debate the subject matter. It trained students
in disciplined thinking, habituated Europeans to great exact-
ness, to careful distinctions, and made the world safe for
reason. The scholastic philosophy laid the foundations upon
which later European thought was to be reared. [72]

        The abstractions of the scholastics found a new chal-
lenge in the philosophers who called themselves "nominalists."
The mental disciplines which had been ousted by dialectic
came back into favor. [73] The first exponent of this nominalist view, it will be recalled, was Roscellinus, the teacher
of Abelard. The most notable medieval example of a synthesis between empiricism and Nominalism was the work of
William of Occam. [74] William of Occam, known as William
Ockham (c1280-1349), with his critical inquiring mentality
demanded logical thought of the "authorities." [75] He had a

revitalizing effect on scholarship.   In contrast with the
scholars who had edited texts, commented on them, discussed
them in accordance with the rules, and whose reasoning had
been based upon the written word and upon unquestioning acceptance of authorities rather than upon observable facts,
Ockham stressed the value of direct experience, encouraging
his followers to observe closely and to experiment. [76] Ockham argued that only empirically observable facts could be
regarded as demonstrable by reason; all else must be regarded as falling within the sphere of faith.   Herein lies the
dim beginning of modern science.   Ockhamist scepticism led
to a concentration on investigation of individual phenomena.
While some of his followers made remarkable discoveries,
these men could not achieve definite results since they
lacked the necessary instruments and experimental techniques.
At least they could formulate problems and pave the way for
their solution by men like Copernicus. [77]

       The nominalist viewpoint, as it gained a foothold,
weakened medieval authoritarianism and initiated the modern
practice of finding facts from first-hand observation.   Particular things became more important than universal forms.
To use their own language, the scholastics reasoned a priori,
while the nominalists did so a posteriori; that is, one reasoned before the fact and the other after the fact.   These
systems approximate the difference between deductive and
inductive thought, the latter leading to the experimental
method of modern science. [78] Definition and classification
were the essence of medieval thinking, wrote Mumford, so
that philosophic Nominalism, which challenged the objective
reality of classes and presented a world of unrelated atoms
and disconnected events, was as destructive to the medieval
style of life as cannonballs proved to be to the walls of the
city. [79] The result of this new mental orientation was to
have important consequences in the realm of art as well as
scientific inquiry.   It was to lead in the next century to the
representation of figures amid natural surroundings, to the
rendering of the body with anatomical accuracy of bone and
muscle, to the modeling of figures in three dimensions by
means of light and shadow, and to the working out of laws
of linear perspective for foreground and background effects.

Scientific Method

       Until versions of the Greek scientific works appeared
in Arabic in the tenth and eleventh centuries and in Latin,

mostly from the Arabic, in the thirteenth and fourteenth centuries, the period beginning with the decline of the Roman
Empire was almost barren in positive scientific results.
The consensus of scholars is that modern science arose in
the fifteenth and sixteenth centuries primarily as a result of
Greek science, and that the active modern period of progressive science extended from about 1450 onward. [80]

The fact that the accumulation of knowledge derived
from the Arabic had involved rapid development in the whole
mental life of Western Europe but brought forth only minute
achievements in experimental science--minute, that is, when
compared with those of the best Greek and Arabic centuries--
indicates the existence of inhibiting factors during those centuries. Although no positive answer can ever be given as to
why the masters at the university did not turn to the verification of their speculations by observation and experiment,
scholars offer two factors for consideration: the fact that
respect for ancient authorities was a basic attitude; and the
predominance of logic in medieval thought. [81] No attempt is
made to analyze these factors; they are considered only in
relation to their effect upon the development of a new teaching method and the role of printing in that development.

The attempt to define "science" raises many difficulties. In the early Middle Ages what has come to be called
"science" was known as "natural philosophy, " and the Latin
word scientia meant nothing more definite than "knowledge. "
The modern usage of the term, on the other hand, covers
only certain kinds of knowledge, an area so vast that no
man can have a grasp of more than a minute fraction of
them. [82] "Science, " for the purposes of this study, is understood to refer to a search for judgments to which universal
assent may be obtained--universal, that is, on the part of
those who understand the judgments and their bases. "Scientific method" refers to the chain of activities described
in the procedure by which knowledge is gained regarding empirical studies. [83] All the various activities and disciplines
implied in the terms "science" and "scientific" involve systematic and unbiased observations, and the examination of
the records of these observations by trained minds leads to
classification, from which classifications general rules or
"laws" are deduced, which may then be applied to further
observations. Failures in correspondence between the new
observations and accepted laws may result in alterations of
laws, and these alterations then lead to further observations,
and so on. This chain of activities and disciplines is under-

stood in this study to constitute in general the "method" of
science. Music, mathematics, and theology, which were included in "science" as the Middle Ages understood it, are
by definition excluded. Admittedly, this chain of activities
is not followed invariably, for it may be short-circuited by
some sort of mental process, but even in such cases the
final appeal is to observation, often in that specialized form
known as experiment. With the spread of the awareness
that science is the making of knowledge and is not knowledge
as such, "science" has become constantly more equated with
"research" and has come to connote a process and not a
static body of doctrine, for when the process of making knowledge ceases, science subsides into static or recessive tradition. [84] This is not to say, however, that science excludes
tradition; conversely, science necessarily involves a developing tradition. Even though cases of research exist wherein
the researcher confines himself temporarily to his own
thoughts, those thoughts have been shaped by the scientific
tradition. The man of science inherits an age-old way of
thinking and his research is but a part of an ever-growing
body of knowledge based upon tradition. [85] Science, then, is
a search that never ends and is never satisfied. Since scientific knowledge is a developing thing, its structure and
functions, as with other developing things, can be understood
only through its history. [86]

Historically, the framework of medieval thought with
its classification of the seven liberal arts into the trivium
and quadrivium, as has been discussed, dates back to the
close of the classical age. The quadrivium provided the
framework for the scientific curriculum which included arithmetic, astronomy, geometry, and music. As was true of
the trivium, the quadrivium up to the twelfth century was
dominated by Boethius. Arithmetic consisted at first of the
simple processes of addition, subtraction, multiplication, and
division. It varied, however, in implication. In Boethius's
De institutione arithmetica it meant the doctrine of the
properties of number, especially of ratio and proportion.
Again, arithmetic meant rules for working the abacus, or
counting-board, by which calculations in money and other
"sums" were solved. The abacus, introduced in the eleventh
century, was equipped with roman numerals at the top of
vertical columns to show the order of units, tens, and hundreds. Arithmetic also usually meant methods for determining Easter and the movable feasts of the Church, particularly in the clergy schools. Here arithmetic was helped
by astronomy. [87] The most popular subject in the quadrivium

was always astronomy, which consisted of instruction on the
course of the sun, the moon, and the stars; also on the
change of seasons, often based upon an outline of practical
astronomy by Bede. In addition to Pliny the Elder's Natural
History, the nearest approach to a text up to the twelfth century was the eighth book of Capella's on the marriage of Philology and Mercury. [88] These were supplemented by the sum-
maries found in the earlier encyclopedias of Isidore of Se-
ville and Rabanus Maurus, and some of the works of Alcuin
and a few others. [89] Astronomy, which never quite emanci-
pated itself from astrology, included such observation as
was possible with rudely constructed instruments. Geometry
before the twelfth century was elementary, for only the
propositions of Euclid without the proofs were available, and
only a few operations such as the calculation of an angle
could be performed with these. The favorite textbook in
geometry was Boethius's Ars geometrica. Traditionally, the
study of geometry also included some rudimentary instruction in geography. [90] Music, the last subject of the quadrivium, was classed by medieval scholars as a theoretical
science, mathematical in character. Along with theories of
music, the playing of instruments was usually studied, and
also the art of choral singing, the latter including the nu-
merical relations of musical sound. The textbook used was
Boethius's De musica. [91]

Although there have been periods in which scientific
progress was retarded or in which its records were forgot-
ten or destroyed, these periods are of interest because of
the fragments of the scientific tradition that survived them.
The influx of Greek scientific works in Arabic, and in Latin
translations from the Arabic resulting from contacts with
the East, stimulated and enriched the knowledge of the physical world. They enlarged the resources available for the
study of the liberal arts and furnished material for new professional courses in the universities whose curricula were
based upon them. [92] Regarding the four traditional disciplines of the quadrivium, arithmetic was now studied in
Moslem treatises, and with the introduction of the zero and
other numerals to Western Europe from the Arabian mathe-
maticians in the twelfth and thirteenth centuries the study of
algorism was made possible; that is, calculation by the nine
integers and zero as now practiced. [93] For geometry, all of
Euclid was recovered in the twelfth and thirteenth centuries
and new Arabic treatises on algebra and trigonometry were
introduced into Western Europe. With these came a revival
of Roman methods of surveying. As a result, students were

taught to compute the areas of triangles and circles and
polygons. In music, advances were being made in the singing schools, possibly under the influence of Moslem music
but much of it by practical experience. 94 Astronomy was
the main interest of the scholastic age, at which stage it
was still not distinguishable from astrology. For astronomy
the twelfth and thirteenth centuries provided Moslem astronomical tables and Ptolemy's Almagest. Ptolemy (fl. A.D.
c140) had provided the final syntheses of Greek science for
cosmology and geography, and his Almagest was of the highest significance for later astronomical development. 95 Although the basic cosmic conceptions of Ptolemy's Almagest
came from his predecessors, they were expounded by Ptolemy
with the utmost skill. The existence of the astronomical instruments which he possessed proves the high degree of me-
chanical skill which had evolved in exact metalwork through
the generations, and they also show how much Ptolemy had
accomplished with them. With these rude instruments
Ptolemy in the second century A.D. was able to determine
the date of the equinoxes, the mid-day altitude of the sun,
the zenith distance of the moon at its meridian passage, the
meridian transit of stars, the apparent diameter of sun or
moon, and the latitude and longitude of the moon or of a
fixed star. Among Ptolemy's greatest achievements was the
determination of the distance of the moon by parallax, which
in principle is the method still in use. This knowledge
along with that in the other great work, his Guide to Geography, which was a product of the knowledge brought to him
by Roman imperial expansion, was passed on to the Middle
Ages. 96

In the study of phenomena, science supplements the
senses by technological devices. The illustrations in these
twelfth- and thirteenth-century works provide an insight into
the nature and the kinds of scientific instruments with which
medieval scholars had to work. A mid-thirteenth century
drawing by Matthew Paris from the Liber experimentarius
of Bernardus Silvestris, Euclid and Hermannus, as illustrated
in the study by Hunt, shows Euclid holding a "sphaera" and
looking through a "dioptra." Beside Euclid sits Hermann of
Corinthia, the medieval translator of several Arabic works
on astronomy, holding an astrolabe. The sphaera appears
to be a globe upon which are drawn astronomical circles,
while the dioptra was not a telescope but simply a hollow
tube used to cut out extraneous light and to measure, by
means of sliding plates inside, the angle and apparent diameter of heavenly bodies. 97 The astrolabe was an instrument

used to observe the positions of the celestial bodies. The
practical results of scholastic astronomical activities were,
however, meager.

The influence of science in any narrow sense cannot
be disentangled from other influences which worked through
all the studies of the history, languages, beliefs, and social
life of mankind. The view of the structure of the universe
as conveyed in these works also provided the medieval world
picture. The earth, which was believed to be of globular
shape, immovably fixed in space, was considered the center
of the universe and the stage for a divinely directed drama.
Around it revolved the celestial spheres, it was believed,
consisting of fire, water, air, and the different constella-
tions and circles of stars. The place of the condemned was
thought to be located in the interior of the globe, while the
dwellings of the blessed in heaven were beyond the starry
circles. As a consequence of the Crusades and commercial
and missionary expeditions, the surface of the earth came
to be better known. [98] The medieval view of the universe
was illustrated in a pen drawing dating about 1200 from the
so-called False Decretals, now in the Bibliothèque Municipale, Rheims, again from the Hunt study. To the medieval
mind all knowledge formed a harmony, and the drawing shows
Harmony personified as the male figure of Air. Air, like
the soul, medieval man believed, "embraces everything between heaven and earth." The figure of Air is shown controlling the four winds, and in the three segments of the
cosmic circle are medallions of the nine Muses. In the
center are shown Arion, personifying literature; Orpheus,
music; and Pythagoras, the sciences. [99]

Medieval thought is thus based upon a classical heritage, and its history is the story of the acceptance, the assimilation, the comprehension, the absorption, the transmu-
tation of that tradition. After the work of translation had
been completed, the problem still remained of assimilating
Greek and Arabic with Christianity. The works of Aristotle
on metaphysics and natural philosophy were too remote from
the medieval ways of thought to be assimilated without more
preparation. This task awaited the thirteenth century and
the accomplishment of Thomas Aquinas. Thus the final synthesis of ideas was slow in emerging. [100] Assimilation and
use of this new knowledge proceeded at a slow rate, one
reason being the lack of Arabic-Latin dictionaries or gram-
mars, which meant that the only way to discover the meaning
of words or the understanding of difficult passages was to

employ the services of an interpreter. Another reason for
the slowness of assimilation was that medieval Latin had no
technical scientific vocabulary, and Arabic words were often
transliterated. Many of the Greek terms had no exact Latin
equivalent, therefore texts were rendered word for word.
This method affected the absorption of the material by medieval scholars because the meaning of texts--Aristotle, as a
case in point--difficult enough to understand in Greek, when
turned into a Latin with Greek constructions became even
more difficult to absorb.[101] While the influx of Greek and
Arabic treatises on the natural sciences focused the attention
of the masters at the University of Paris upon these disciplines and opened up new fields for study, inquiry, and speculation, they at the same time inhibited progress by providing
texts which were material for argument.[102]

The problems which the new learning created affected
the development of a scientific method in two important ways.
First, much of the intellectual energy of the thirteenth-century scholars was absorbed in explaining, clarifying, ration-
alizing, looking for common causes and principles. Secondly,
from 1230 on the influence of Greek and Arabic thought resulted in a marked increase in theological speculation.[103]
Although the spirit of scientific inquiry was alive and active,
as will be seen, it was of subordinate importance in the
general scheme of thought.

The curriculum of the University of Paris gave no
place to experimental science, nor did its organization into
"faculties" provide for a faculty of science. For the degree
of Master of Arts not much more was yet needed than a
thorough knowledge of the chief works of Aristotle.[104] On
the other hand, the thirteenth century did show progress in
the accuracy of scientific observation and in the empirical
collection and classification of scientific facts and data.
Scientific experiments of importance had been made, it is
true, scattered over two or three centuries. Experiments
had been made with the compass, perhaps under Arabian influence; the problem of the path of light within a spherical
lens was partially solved on a mathematical basis; a para-
bolic burning mirror was constructed, or at least attempted;
the study of optics had resulted in a correct understanding
of the phenomenon of the rainbow; a solitary genius had
made a complex but workable astronomical clock. These
achievements, however, were minor when compared with
those of the best Greek or Arabic centuries.[105] Notable
among those who made significant contributions to scientific

knowledge are Albert Magnus, teacher of Thomas Aquinas, known as Albert the Great; Robert Grosseteste, and his famous pupil, Roger Bacon.

Albert Magnus (1193-1280), who was trained and taught at the University of Paris, recognized that the Milky Way consisted of a multitude of stars; he discussed the influence of the axial direction of mountain ranges on climatic conditions; and, using the empirical method of Aristotle, he observed animal organisms and plants minutely and produced accurate descriptions of them. [106] Albert Magnus held in principle that "natural science does not consist in ratifying what others have said, but in seeking out the causes of phenomena."[107] Although he did observe natural phenomena and incorporated his observations in his work, Albert Magnus did not test the opinions of others by experiment. [108] Robert Grosseteste (1175-1253) and Roger Bacon (1214?-1292) both made contributions to knowledge in fields where little equipment was needed, such as optics and astronomy, through observation and some understanding of the value of the inductive as well as the deductive method. [109] Grosseteste, through the translations of Arabic scientific works into Latin, became familiar with the most advanced knowledge in mathematics and astronomy. His special interest was optics, in which field his famous pupil Roger Bacon did some of his most valuable work. In his work on optics, as quoted in Hunt's study, Roger Bacon wrote:

> I shall draw therefore a figure in which all these matters are made clear as far as possible as a surface, though the full demonstration would require a body fashioned like the eye in all the particulars aforesaid. The eye of a cow, pig or other animal can be used for illustration, if anyone wishes to experiment. [110]

His work, too, depended upon the mastery of a text. Roger Bacon's statement formulates the attitude of medieval scholars toward authorities: "When one knows the text, one knows all that concerns the science which is the object of the text."[111]

The thirteenth century, then, was aware of the experimental method, which associates logic and mathematics with direct experience. In the study of scientific subjects, observation played some part and the testing of hypotheses by experiment was not unknown. Although a fertile field of

research was thus opened, this method was scarcely exploited at the time, for it is a long step from making observations to the formulation of a theoretical basis of experi-
mentation, and the climate where authorities counted for so
much did not favor it.[112] In general, science was learned
and taught in much the same way as the other subjects.
Earlier teaching method concentrated upon emphasizing facts
to be memorized and given back in recitation. In the thirteenth century, the Aristotelian science was the best yet
known in the world, and that is why Thomas Aquinas thought
it was necessary to integrate it with Christian revelation.
Since it was based upon a system of deductive reasoning
from certain premises, however, it was basically an intellectual "blind alley."[113] The deductive method and the technique of disputation applied to these physical sciences did
little to further them.[114]

Although the scholars of the later Middle Ages added
little to the growth of the scientific heritage, they did contribute toward its coherence and presentation.[115] The great
scholars of the universities, particularly of the University
of Paris, set a standard of scrupulously methodical thought.
The orientation of medieval thought was altered through the
interaction of various forces over a long stretch of time,
but the decisive period was the century between 1450 and
1550. During this time much of the scientific heritage had
been recovered, and this century also saw the introduction
and spread of the arts of printing and illustration, both of
major importance for scientific development.[116] The study
of ancient Greek writers not only equipped scholars with
better textbooks, but it also set new problems which men of
action could not solve for themselves. The new facts would
not have been assimilated and the new problems would not
have been tackled if there had not already been in existence
an organized system of thought and education.[117] Hypotheses
were developed both by reasoning and by experimental tryout.
Definitions, laws, and theories were derived, and not accepted on authority. Modern scientific knowledge resulted
from this reform in logic. The new science had two advantages: first, it had a better empirical technology, the
product of the medieval centuries; and secondly, it was aided
by a method of exposition which was a real contribution of
scholastic thought.[118]

A herald of the "new philosophy" or modern science
at the transition between medieval and modern thought was
Francis Bacon (1561-1626).[119] With Francis Bacon, a new

approach to knowledge, a new method of knowing emerged.
In his Novum Organum, he presented the method of inductive
verification of hypotheses. Knowing and learning started not
with acceptance of a stated definition or law by the student,
but with observation of the world around him. Scrutiny of
the facts and of the problems related to those facts called
for the development of hypotheses to guide the search for
further facts.[120] As a result of Francis Bacon's work, the
inductive process now stood alongside the deductive. The
method of teaching ultimately based on this new development
directed students to observation and analysis of phenomena
in the world, with comparisons over a series of specific in-
stances leading to generalization.[121] The pen drawing from
the False Decretals, previously referred to, in which Harmony was personified, illustrates the way by which facts
were chosen and interpreted in the Middle Ages; that is, according to theological systems rather than being collected
empirically for their own sake. The new method called for
quite different mental activities on the part of scientific man,
which included the four processes of collecting observations,
forming an hypothesis that links the observations, testing the
truth or falsehood of the hypothesis, and using the hypothesis
in examination of further observations or re-examination of
those already considered. When the hypothesis answers suit-
ably to repeated or sufficiently delicate tests, the scientist
has found new knowledge: he has made a discovery.[122]

While the study of the philosophy and history of science
makes the world more worthy of investigation, absorbing the
reader and raising the status of the man of science, such
study will never be a direct instrument of discovery, scholars point out. Examination of fragments of learning cannot
reveal the processes of the development of science.[123]
Being composed to convince the reader of certain views or
to put him in possession of certain knowledge, texts normal-
ly obscure the process, consisting of working hypotheses in-
terspersed with a provisional series of observations, by
which such views were reached. Many of the judgments may
have been untenable and many observations irrelevant, ill-
chosen, or needing further test. A textbook or treatise
would necessarily omit these side issues and false starts because if it did not, it would be too diffuse. These omissions,
however, conceal the sequence of events leading to the new
knowledge or discovery. Textbooks or reliance upon authorities alone, therefore, are inadequate in following the new
method, for they give a false impression of the process.
For this reason, among others, science cannot be learned

from books alone, but only by contact with actual phenomena. [124] This is not to imply that textbooks are not necessary
to the new method; on the contrary, research is but part of
an ever-growing body of knowledge based upon tradition. It
would imply, however, that the medieval dependence upon
texts was one deterrent in the development of the experimental method. With regard to tradition, Auguste Comte is
quoted as saying, "The history of science is science itself."[125]

The characteristic of the modern scientific scene which
separates it from the medieval is less possession of a method than devotion to observation as the demonstrative test.
Scientific elements existed among medieval activities but, with
little devotion to observation, they produced few results.
The scientific process, then, may be further reduced to two
main activities: discovery and demonstration. Regarding discovery, ideas used by scientific man in his inquiry into the
phenomena of nature have reached him through various ways--
from a dream, an illuminating flash, a painful calculation,
through suggestion by an analogy--all of which are matters
of temperament and human individuality.   It is in the process
of demonstration, then, that man's efforts may be discerned
as scientific.   Demonstration makes the science. [126] During
the Middle Ages, the relationship between the process of discovery and that of demonstration was almost consistently
avoided.   Francis Bacon makes no mention of this relationship. [127] Although he did emphasize the importance of systematic fact collection, he failed to perceive how deeply the
act of judgment must be involved in it.   In his Advancement
of Learning, Francis Bacon set forth the belief that in any
field of knowledge the facts might be collected according to
an accepted and prearranged plan and then passed through an
automatic logical process from which correct judgments
would inevitably emerge.   This method cannot be applied in
practice, since phenomena are beyond number.   Therefore,
when any field of knowledge is to be explored, it is necessary
for the scientist to choose from among phenomena or facts.
The question which then arises is how the scientist can best
choose the phenomena to be observed and recorded. [128] The
process of choosing phenomena represents an act of judgment
on the part of a learned or experienced chooser, a scientist.
The choice of the scientist is necessarily controlled by knowledge of his special field.   The successful scientific man,
while he may be directed by training, is fully acquainted with
the history of his field or subject.   He is always molded by
tradition.   The history of science shows that only those with
a knowledge of how their predecessors have succeeded or

failed have chosen profitably.   The scientific tradition thus
has its place in the new method, for science, insofar as it
is a live and a developing thing, can build only upon the
science that has gone before.   Thus, while an exclusive dependence upon texts was a deterrent, the use of texts in the
scientific method cannot be profitably eliminated.[129]

Notes

1. Mumford, op. cit., p. 275.

2. Douglas, op. cit., p. 190.

3. Genicot, op. cit., p. 188.

4. Mumford, op. cit., p. 276.

5. Pacaut, op. cit., p. 305.

6. William Henry Burton, "Methods of Teaching, " Encyclopaedia Britannica (1964 ed.), XXI, 866B.

7. Douglas, op. cit., p. 189.

8. Thompson and Johnson, op. cit., p. 726.

9. Mâle, op. cit., pp. 76-77.

10. Ibid., p. 67.

11. Ibid., p. 77.

12. Ibid., p. 79.

13. Ibid.

14. Ibid.

15. Ibid., pp. 78-79, citing Martianus Capella, The Mar-
    riage of Philology and Mercury.

16. Ibid., p. 78.

17. Ibid.

18. Ibid., p. 79.

19. Hunt, op. cit., p. 196.

20. Ibid.

21. Southern, op. cit., p. 175.

22. Ibid., p. 174.

23. Artz, op. cit., p. 309.

24. Reinhardt, op. cit., p. 141.

25. Burton, op. cit., p. 866B.

26. Hunt, op. cit., p. 197.

27. Ibid.

28. Artz, op. cit., p. 310.

29. Thompson and Johnson, op. cit., p. 733.

30. Ibid., p. 723.

31. Marshall McLuhan, The Gutenberg Galaxy (Toronto: University of Toronto Press, 1965), p. 109.

32. Putnam, op. cit., I, 216.

33. Hunt, op. cit., p. 200.

34. Powicke, op. cit., p. 170.

35. Artz, op. cit., p. 307.

36. Ernest Barker, "Aristotle," Encyclopaedia Britannica (1964 ed.), II, 395.

37. "Scholasticism" Encyclopaedia Britannica (1964 ed.), XX, 81.

38. Ibid., p. 82.

39. Barker, op. cit., p. 395.

40. Ibid., p. 394.

41. Burton, op. cit., p. 866B.

42. Evans, op. cit., pp. 106-7.

43. Ibid., p. 105.

44. Genicot, op. cit., p. 159.

45. Fremantle and others, op. cit., p. 97.

46. Hunt, op. cit., p. 197.

47. Southern, op. cit., p. 176.

48. Hunt, op. cit., p. 197.

49. C. G. Crump and E. F. Jacob, The Legacy of the
    Middle Ages (Oxford: The Clarendon Press, 1948),
    p. 272.

50. Albert Léon Guérard, French Civilization (New York:
    Cooper Square Publishers, Inc., 1969), p. 202.

51. Hunt, op. cit., p. 197.

52. Southern, op. cit., p. 181.

53. Fremantle and others, op. cit., p. 97.

54. Reinhardt, op. cit., p. 146.

55. Stephenson, op. cit., p. 268.

56. Southern, op. cit., p. 182.

57. Reinhardt, op. cit., p. 143.

58. Hunt, op. cit., p. 196.

59. Genicot, op. cit., p. 159.

60. Evans, op. cit., p. 107.

61. Crump and Jacob, op. cit., p. 274.

62. Putnam, op. cit., I, 261.

63. Guérard, op. cit., p. 200.

64. Crump and Jacob, op. cit., p. 274.

65. "History of Education, " Encyclopaedia Britannica (1964
     ed.), VII, 987.

66. Guérard, op. cit., p. 206.

67. Stephenson, op. cit., p. 265.

68. Cantor, op. cit., p. 504.

69. Starr and others, op. cit., I, 490.

70. Evans, op. cit., p. 103.

71. Starr and others, op. cit., I, 490.

72. Ibid.

73. Genicot, op. cit., p. 246.

74. David Francis Pears, "Nominalism, " Encyclopaedia
     Britannica (1964 ed.), XVI, 482.

75. Eligius M. Buytaert, "William of Occam, " Encyclo-
     paedia Britannica (1964 ed.), XVI, 680.

76. Genicot, op. cit., p. 242.

77. Morrall, op. cit., p. 139.

78. Fleming, op. cit., p. 228.

79. Mumford, op. cit., p. 304.

80. Charles Singer, "Science, " Encyclopaedia Britannica
     (1964 ed.) XX, 119-20.

81. Hunt, op. cit., p. 200.

82. Singer, op. cit., p. 114.

83. William Calvert Kneale, "Scientific Method, " Encyclo-
     paedia Britannica (1964 ed.), XX, 126.

84. Singer, op. cit., p. 114.

85. Ibid.

86. Ibid., p. 115.

87. Crump and Jacob, op. cit., p. 272.

88. Hunt, op. cit., p. 196.

89. Thompson and Johnson, op. cit., p. 726.

90. Artz, op. cit., p. 310.

91. Ibid.

92. Singer, op. cit., p. 119.

93. Crump and Jacob, op. cit., p. 273.

94. Thompson and Johnson, op. cit., p. 727.

95. Singer, op. cit., p. 119.

96. Ibid.

97. Hunt, op. cit., p. 198, citing Bernardus Silvestris, Euclid and Hermannus, Liber experimentarius (MS Ashmole 304, fol. 2V, in the Bodleian Library, Oxford, mid-thirteenth century).

98. Reinhardt, op. cit., p. 120.

99. Hunt, op. cit., p. 198, citing False Decretals (MS 672 in the Bibliothèque Municipale, Rheims, c1200).

100. Genicot, op. cit., p. 185.

101. Hunt, op. cit., p. 198.

102. Genicot, op. cit., p. 187.

103. Ibid., p. 185.

104. Crump and Jacob, op. cit., p. 275.

105. Singer, op. cit., p. 120.

106. Reinhardt, op. cit., p. 140.

107. Genicot, op. cit., p. 187.

108. Starr and others, op. cit., I, 492.

109. Cantor, op. cit., p. 512.

110. Hunt, op. cit., p. 201, citing Roger Bacon, Optics
      (MS in the British Museum, late thirteenth cen-
      tury).

111. Putnam, op. cit., I, 216.

112. Hunt, op. cit., p. 200.

113. Cantor, op. cit., p. 512.

114. Genicot, op. cit., p. 187.

115. Singer, op. cit., p. 119.

116. Ibid., p. 120.

117. George Clark, Early Modern Europe (New York: Ox-
      ford University Press, 1960), p. 162.

118. Singer, op. cit., p. 120.

119. "Francis Bacon," Encyclopaedia Britannica (1964 ed.),
      II, 993.

120. Burton, op. cit., p. 866B.

121. Ibid.

122. Singer, op. cit., p. 115.

123. Ibid.

124. Ibid., p. 114.

125. Ibid.

126. Ibid., p. 115.

127. Ibid.

128. <u>Ibid</u>.

129. <u>Ibid</u>.

Chapter 7

BOOK PRODUCTION

While clearly there may be many different methods by which scientists gain knowledge in different fields of research, the focus in this study is upon the inductive method of teaching which had emerged with the modern science of the fifteenth and sixteenth centuries based upon observation and experiment. The method of teaching is of interest in this study primarily because of the role of printing in the development of the scientific method, the effect of printing upon the volume of book production in the sixteenth century, and the effect of the increased volume resulting from the printing method of book production upon the physical expansion of the city of Paris. The topic of book production, therefore, is subdivided into printing, publishing, and volume of production.

Printing

The subjects selected for discussion here, as they relate to the role of printing in the development of the scientific method and the subsequent effect of printing upon book production, are perspective and illustration, accuracy of text, oral techniques, dependence upon authorities, apparatus of learning, and libraries.

The spirit of free inquiry was not confined to the intellectual life of the University of Paris. It permeated all the progressive aspects of life. In the fifteenth century it led to a new experimental attitude and a new concept of space. A close relationship developed between art and science.[1] This close relationship facilitated the transition to the inductive method of teaching. The impulse to take the image of things and by representation to make them part of the mind that perceived them came to a focus in the early years of the fifteenth century in the Burgundian court of the Duke of Berry, who surrounded himself with the

greatest artists and book illuminators of the time. Among
them was Pol de Limbourg, who, with his brothers, painted
the illustrations for The Très Riches Heures.[2] The Très
Riches Heures shows that the interest had gradually shifted
from the best way of telling a sacred story as clearly and
impressively as possible to the methods of representing an
object of nature in the most faithful way.[3]

The Limbourgs, champions of a pictorial Nominalism,[4]
were at this time in the midst of great discoveries about the
world and the means of representing it. They were innovators. With the Limbourgs, the medieval tradition of stylized
landscape with figures placed against a flat gold background
was definitely abandoned in favor of greater naturalism.
They developed simultaneously the portraiture of persons and
of their environment. The Limbourgs could not yet represent the space in which their figures moved, and the illusion
of reality was achieved mainly through close attention to detail.[5] By the imaginative selection of subject and setting, by
the sensitive use of light and color and a vivid sense of
space and atmosphere, the Limbourgs depict in this handwritten manuscript the occupations of the different seasons of
the year with a wealth of detail and careful attention to the
correct representation of man-made and natural objects.[6]
The miniature of "May," for example, with all the colorful
pageantry of the annual spring festival of the courtiers, its
musicians leading the gay group of amiable riders to the
sound of trumpet, flute, trombone, was, it is believed,
painted with a magnifying glass.[7] Again, the people and
boats reflected in the water and the shadows cast on the
ground in the miniature of "October" are the earliest known
representations of such phenomena. Here too, in the enor-
mous, four-square Louvre, the linear perspective of the Limbourgs, although not fully systematic, helps to create imposing masses.[8]

It was the nominalist viewpoint which, as noted above,
weakened medieval authoritarianism and initiated the practice
of finding facts from first-hand observation. This new viewpoint found expression in art. From the naturalism of the
fourteenth century its more scientific equivalent developed in
the fifteenth, which led in the sixteenth century to the rendering of the body with anatomical accuracy of bone and muscle, to the modeling of figures in three dimensions by means
of light and shadow, and to the working out of laws of linear
perspective for foreground and background effects.[9]

The main technical instrument of Renaissance art was perspective. This new device is truly scientific because, given certain conditions, its truth can be demonstrated experimentally and its accuracy estimated.[10] Although Leonardo da Vinci (1452-1519) was its greatest scientific exponent, it was the product of many minds.[11] Perspective influenced many sciences. All developments involving geometry in three dimensions, for example, became more easily intelligible. More importantly, it made possible the adequate representations of living things and their parts. For the first time, many details of the structure of human and animal bodies could be made clear on paper. In the first half of the sixteenth century, this same movement which linked the study of nature with sceintific perspective produced many exact studies of plant form.[12] Although sixteenth-century science was still influenced by the emphasis upon pseudosciences such as astrology, alchemy, demonology, and was still handicapped by dependence upon ancient authorities, nevertheless, a minority of anatomists, botanists and physicists contributed to the observation and classification of natural phenomena by experimenting for themselves. Thus they provided a starting place for the scientific innovators of the next century. The first scientific monograph in the modern manner to appear was the De Humanis Corporis Fabrica (On the Fabric of the Human Body), by Andreas Vesalius. Vesalius, whose work was based upon the work of Galen in the second century A.D., performed hundreds of anatomical experiments and rejected Galen wherever he found a conflict. Prior to Vesalius, anatomists had ignored experimental evidence that disagreed with Galen.[13] Vesalius employed all the resources of the art of his age, hiring artists to illustrate his personal observations.[14] Another resource which Vesalius utilized was the art of printing. His book was published in 1543.

Although scientific treatises in the late medieval and early Renaissance period were illustrated with great care and a real attempt was made to portray exactly the objects under consideration, this was hindered by the impossibility of accurately multiplying pictures. In the handwritten manuscript, reproduction of which meant having scores of scribes copying drawings rather than drawing from life, the artist's work was likely to be distorted beyond recognition, no matter how careful the original drawing of plant or animal. Only with the invention of printing in the first half of the fifteenth century and its introduction into Paris in the latter half did it become possible for illustrations to be exactly reproduced once they had been rendered to the artist's satisfaction. Once a picture was prepared for printing it could be repeated an indefinite number of times with little loss in detail, accuracy, or form.[15]

The use of printed illustrations by fifteenth-century printers produced a new means of expression, offering an excellent opportunity for the faithful reproduction of pictures and diagrams in scientific books. The process had great potential, and it was expertly exploited in the anatomical books of Vesalius. With their adaptability for fine lines, engravings were particularly suitable for the reproduction of maps. One of the few incunabula illustrated with engravings is Ptolemy's Geographia, printed in 1478.[16] Observation was helped by printing. The work of Vesalius, again as a case in point, influenced other anatomists and physicians who benefited from his observations. One illustration, for example, shows the author demonstrating the dissection of an arm.[17] Not only did scientific scholarship benefit from the development of printed illustrations, but new possibilities were also opened in the arts. Painters and sculptors gained invaluable knowledge from these detailed personal observations. Michelangelo learned from the engravings of Schongauer, Andrea del Sarto from Dürer's, and Dürer from Mantegna's engravings.[18] The illustrator came to serve the scholar, and carefully prepared engravings assumed as much importance as the text.

Modern science did not begin with the artists, however; it began at Paris in the classrooms and studies in the crowded, narrow, straw-covered streets of the Latin Quarter, and the way to it was prepared by men who argued over logical terms, pored over the text of Aristotle and gradually came to realize how important it was to observe facts for themselves. Since teaching at the University of Paris depended for its orderly conduct upon the use of authoritative textbooks, the introduction of printing was first appreciated, important though the illustrations were, for the promotion of the certainty of learning. This was particularly true in Paris where the first press was set up within the confines of the Sorbonne.[19] Certainty of learning was dependent, among other factors, upon the technical accuracy of reproduction of the text and upon the authenticity of that text.

Before the introduction of printing, dependable uniform texts were difficult to achieve. Medieval scholars were dependent upon scribes. Each copyist wrote a distinct hand;

each permitted himself endless variations in the formation of
letters and in methods of abbreviating words or shortening
them by other conventions such as suspension of final syl-
lables. Writing under great pressure, the professional scribe
was often careless, and the handwriting itself became poorer
in quality. The more times a manuscript was copied, the
less authentic it became. Although the university formulated
strict regulations for the stationarii who supplied the texts,
deterioration of the text was intensified with the number of
copies made. No two texts were alike. Whatever the pre-
cautions taken to secure authentic texts, the publication of a
work was always liable to involve the multiplication of errors,
and these errors had a cumulative effect. [20]

     In addition to the inaccuracies caused by reproduction
of texts, errors in authenticity were compounded by the students' misunderstanding of the lecturer. One year's class
would have one set of glosses or commentaries which had
been taken down on their wax tablets and later copied, and
another year's class of the same master would have at least
a different emphasis. [21] With the printed book came uniform-
ity and repeatability. The experience of Professor Fichet is
representative. One of the first works edited for publication
in Paris was a copy of the lectures to students entitled
Rhetoric by Guillaume Fichet, a professor at the university
and later rector and librarian of the Sorbonne, who was associated with the introduction of printing into Paris. Having
discovered that copies of his lectures were in circulation
which had been written out from notes taken down by students who had not understood correctly what he said, Fichet
took steps to have it printed under his own watchful supervision. The lectures had contained misstatements that were
far from anything that the lecturer had intended to say.
Fichet wrote joyfully to the prior of the University of Paris
about the new opportunity of using print to banish the "plague
of barbarously copied texts."[22]

     Gutenberg's invention proved itself a practical solu-
tion to the problems of reproduction, whether they concerned
errors in illustration or text or authenticity. When a volume
was printed instead of being copied by hand, it was first
carefully examined. Standards of correctness became more
exacting. In print, with careful composition and careful
proofreading, with the lists of errata and corrections published at once and then incorporated in later reprints, a high
standard of accuracy was achieved. Perfection was the goal
of many of the great printers of the sixteenth century and of

their successors.[23]

Prominent in this notable period was a family of
scholar printers, the house of Estienne. The chief products
of the press of Henry Estienne, the first of the family, were
Greek and Latin classics addressed to an academic circle of
readers. The high scholarly character of his work was continued by Robert Estienne, who in 1524 at the age of twenty-
one took over the paternal printing office and put to good
use the instruction of his stepfather, Simon de Colines. The
house of Estienne contributed not a little to making the first
sixty years of the sixteenth century in Paris the golden age
of typography. The university authorities assumed from the
first the responsibility to supervise the series of operations
by which university texts were prepared and circulated. The
close supervision of the Sorbonne extended to every aspect
of the textbook business, from the correctness and neatness
of the texts to the lists of titles kept in stock, to the number
of copies of each on hand, to the prices charged for the loan
and sale of these books. Since the sustained and active interest of the Sorbonne in all these matters had an impact
upon book production, the subject of censorship and regulation, and also of the scholar printers, will be discussed
within the context of publishing.

The scarcity of handwritten manuscripts and the high
cost of their reproduction accounted in part for the use of
the lecture technique and the exposition of standard textbooks by the masters of the early Middle Ages. Science, it
has been noted, was in general taught much the same as the
other subjects. Discussion, too, was natural in a community of men and boys with few books but with many opportunities for meeting together; indeed, discussion was a necessity in the days of the wax tablet and the pooling of lecture
notes. The medieval method of teaching with its lectures,
discussion, memorization, scholastic philosophy or dialectic,
was deeply oral in its procedures and orientation. This
lecture technique of teaching was broken down by a number
of factors, not the least of which was the printing press.
By the sixteenth century, books could be produced more
quickly, more inexpensively, and in greater quantities.
With the increase in the quantity of production and the availability of the printed book, the number of readers was increased. As a result, the influence of the writers grew.
More books were to be had in the universities and so the
more personal influence of the master gave way before the
might of the printed book and its unseen author. Learning,

which had been circumscribed by the limitations of the master
and the boundaries of available knowledge, expanded in
scope. [24]

The content of books was marked by a serious consideration of events and experiences which had not been reported in earlier books. The new in thought of the sixteenth
century was exceptionally different from the old, three of the
forces bringing about the new information being the geographical discoveries, the Renaissance, and the Reformation. Histories, for example, recovered the interest in common details; biographies recounted the lives of those below the rank
or degree of saint, pope, emperor, king; chronicles appeared
to report a limited but immediate account of daily events;
travelers told of different peoples and cultures. The significant point about these developments is the serious interest
taken by scholars in all kinds of subjects. The enlarged
content of books reflected a changed approach to knowledge
which continued the shift away from medieval otherworldli-
ness, emphasizing in contrast the reality of sensual experience. This revised attitude attributed great importance to
observation and experience as avenues of learning. [25] Personal observation of the physical world gradually replaced
authoritarian and purely deductive reasoning in viewing the
world. The scientific promise of the sixteenth century had
to wait for another age to be fully realized, however. Contributions of the sixteenth-century scientists to the observation and classification of natural phenomena provided the
starting place for the achievements of scientific innovators
of the following century. [26] With the improved empirical
technology and with the method of exposition characteristic
of scholastic thought which the medieval centuries bequeathed
to posterity, the great exponents of scientific method of the
seventeenth century could proceed with their work.

Since the whole field of experience far exceeded the
capacity of any individual master, the new approach to knowledge was reflected in books--not only scientific knowledge,
but the whole range of life and thought reported in print.
The printers of the sixteenth century disseminated, along
with the old texts, the work of talented new authors. These
authors often channeled their new ideas not only into books,
but into digests, pamphlets, anthologies and florilegia, or
collections of brief extracts and writings. The pace of intellectual change quickened. [27] Novelty, together with the
interaction of other factors, eventually challenged the basic
attitude of respect for and dependence upon ancient authori-

ties. With the coming of the printed book, the day of the
man of one book had ended; the day of the wax tablet had
also ended.

The use of printing also effected a change in the kinds
of books produced. Bringing together many books in one
place such as a university meant that masses of information
could be assembled quickly, which brought about changes in
what has been called the "apparatus" of learning. The
printers put at the disposal of students great books of reference such as dictionaries, encyclopedias, histories, and
collections of texts which, handwritten, could not have been
gathered in a lifetime. [28] An increasing number of books
and other materials were published which added to the con-
veniences of scholars. Published tables of logarithms and
other tabulated mathematical and astronomical material
speeded up scientific calculation. Hand-copied music depended upon skills which the amateur could not be expected
to possess, and the engraved music of the printer provided
the equivalent in accurate, legible, and convenient form.
The printing of music disseminated the latest songs and compositions among the student body. [29] By the end of the sixteenth century, the amount of reading required of a scholar
was greatly expanded and the speculation among scholars is
that the seventeenth century finally ended the medieval custom of reading everything aloud, for only by reading silently
could a person read fast enough to absorb it all. [30] With
printing, the visual intensity of the written page was increased. The printed book with its printed illustrations
was designed by the writer for the reader: both saw it silently on the printed page. [31]

One result of the availability of printed textbooks was
that the focal point of university life shifted from the pre-
occupation with disputation and dialectic to the storehouse
where books were kept. The library became the place to
which both students and faculty went to study. The library
became the core around which a community learning together
organized its academic life.

Publishing

All the new scientific, artistic, and literary activity
characteristic of the fifteenth and sixteenth centuries gave
expression to itself in books. Book illustration attracted the
talents of the greatest artists in the world, and Paris at-

tracted the artists. With the fifteenth century began an unbroken tradition of fine illustration at Paris which has lasted
to the present day. No other city, not even Venice, wrote
Hofer, can boast of so continuous a flow of fine books, one
reason being that Paris has always been one of the largest
and richest cities of Europe and continuously the capital of
one of its greatest powers. [32]

When printing was introduced into Paris about 1470,
it merely accelerated a publishing movement which had developed in the thirteenth and fourteenth centuries. [33] Publishing, as used in this study, refers to the selection, reproduction, and circulation of written matter; thus it is older
than both printing and paper. [34] During the early Middle
Ages, the monasteries were the publishing houses, but from
the second half of the thirteenth century the demand for
manuscripts grew steadily and the monasteries were unable
to cope with it alone. Increased demand brought changes in
both the manuscripts produced and the production process itself. With the growth of universities, the demand increased
for quicker and cheaper production, and gradually paper came
to be used as well as parchment. Manuscripts covered a
wider range of subjects. The book of hours, giving the
prayers for laymen for each hour of the day, made its first
appearance in France in the first half of the fourteenth century. Breviaries made for bishops and popes were similar
in layout and richness of material. [35] Guilds of lay scribes
and miniaturists were being formed in the towns, and by the
time that printing was introduced into Paris, the great
masters working for great patrons had left the field to these
lay miniaturists, who had started to write and illuminate
books of hours as a trade, producing large quantities of such
volumes for the wealthy bourgeoisie. The rise of lay miniaturists foreshadowed the eventual decay of what was essentially a religious art. It was kept alive for a time until
printing, woodcuts and copper engravings completely replaced
illuminated manuscripts. Printed books could be produced
less expensively, more quickly, and in greater numbers to
meet the steadily growing demand. The most important
scriptoria disappeared with the secularization of many monasteries. As printing gradually took over the production of
liturgical books, it robbed illumination of its raison d'etre.
After one last great period shortly after 1500, manuscript
illumination entered a slow and final decline. [36]

France led in manuscript illumination throughout the
Gothic period, and the art was centered on Paris where it

was fostered by the court and the university, both of which commissioned work and financed the training of young artists. Artists flocked into Paris from every direction, not only those of French stock but also Mosans, Rhinelanders, Italians, and Flemish. What attracted them were the commissions of rich collectors who vied with one another in the acquisition of their masterpieces, the most opulent of whom took the finest of the artists into their personal service. Among these artists were Pol from Limbourg and his two brothers who produced one of the richest books of hours, The Très Riches Heures, aforementioned. [37]

Actually, that sphere of manuscript production and illumination had little to do with the manuscript production going on at the University of Paris. The textbook trade of Paris owed its origin to the university. From the thirteenth throughout all of the sixteenth century, the whole book business of the university had no status whatever in the commercial and industrial structure of France, at least theoretically. It was an integral part of the educational system. [38] Two and a half centuries before the introduction of printing, the book trade of the University of Paris had become for the most part the book trade of the city. Moreover, during much of this time Paris shared with Florence the position as center of the intellectual activities of Europe. As the fame of Paris and its university spread, its book-producing population was preparing textbooks not only for the university community, but also literature for the scholarly readers of Paris, of France, and of Europe. [39] The printed volume inherited the manuscript publishing tradition and machinery, and the printed volume traveled immediately along the well-worn paths of the manuscript trade. The book trade was held to include all the dealers and artisans who were concerned with the production and distribution of manuscripts. In Paris all of these booksellers, parchment dealers, copyists, papermakers, and binders were administrative officers or employees of the university. [40]

Since the development of the printing industry was shaped by the manuscript publishing tradition and the privileges as well as the exactions of controls imposed upon it, the following discussion is presented as an historical background to that medieval book trade generated by the University of Paris, its purpose, its privileges, its controls, regulations and censorship. To discuss the technicalities of these privileges and controls is beyond the scope of this study, and consideration of them is limited to their effect upon the vol-

ume of printed book production in the sixteenth century, and
the concomitant effect upon the expansion of the physical
boundaries of the city of Paris.

According to accepted theory, the sole purpose for
the existence of the book trade was to secure for the members of the university a sufficient supply, at a fixed and
moderate charge, of correct and complete texts of the prescribed works; and it was also essential to protect those
members from the contamination of heretical writings or of
heretical comments on books of accepted orthodoxy. [41]

A combination of several factors created a demand
for books before the introduction of printing into Paris. The
factors selected for discussion within this economic context
as they affected demand and supply include the following:
the large student enrollment at the University of Paris, the
technique of instruction, the fame of a master, and the enlarged content of books, all of which have already been introduced.

A vast number of students were congregated together
by the foundation of the University of Paris, a community
ranging in number from ten thousand to as high as thirty
thousand in the days of the University's prime. [42] This large
student body generated a proportionate demand for books.
The lecture technique, characterized by dependence upon the
authorities, and the limited curriculum based upon the trivium and quadrivium did not call for a large supply of books
on the part of the masters in the early decades of the university's existence. If a master needed books other than
those he owned, he might obtain them by borrowing. Toward
this end, a council at Paris in 1212 impressed upon monasteries their duty to lend books as an act of mercy. Evidence of their cooperation exists in a fragmentary catalog
of books found in the binding of a manuscript which seems
to be the remains of an early type of union catalog of a collection of the catalogs in the monasteries of Paris. [43] On
the other hand, the nature of the instruction at the University
of Paris, where authors prescribed and approved were read
and glossed, meant that considerable numbers of texts were
needed by the students. Since education was entirely dependent upon books, this close adherence to the text secured an
assured demand for texts on the part of the students. [44] The
existing supply of texts was inadequate, and the university required that students present themselves at their classes furnished with books they had made; and if that was not possible,

that at least there be a book shared among every three students.[45] Some scholars believe that the book trade in Paris dates from Abelard's time. His immense popularity and tremendous following of students created a demand for books, about which his mortal enemy Saint Bernard resentfully commented: "His books have wings. They leap the Alps."[46] In the thirteenth century the University of Paris was exceptional. Its renowned masters came from all parts of Western Europe, and distinctions of nationality were meaningless, for all were citizens of that international Christian commonwealth, the intellectual capital of which was the University of Paris. The fame of a great master was no longer spread entirely or even mainly by his teaching, but increasingly by his books.[47] With the University of Paris being international in organization and scope, with lines of communication highly developed, with Latin the common language understandable by the majority of readers, intellectual intercourse rapidly reached the limits of the known world. Traveling along the same routes, the manuscript trade became international, recognizing no national frontiers.[48] The demand for books was increased by the widening of the market. The influx of Greek and Arabic texts brought about an expansion of the curriculum. The diversity inherent in the new approach to knowledge and the increased importance of individual writers enlarged the content of books.[49] Since this new knowledge far exceeded the capacity of any individual, the new approach to knowledge was reflected in books and contributed to the demand for books. While other factors in society also contributed, the demand for books in the fourteenth and fifteenth centuries multiplied to the extent that the introduction of printing was the only ultimate method of producing a supply to meet the demand.[50]

In the earliest days, when the book trade had as its purpose to provide prescribed textbooks, the university as a publisher, but not a commercial one, strove to keep prices down for the students by encouraging the use of old copies, which also relieved the university of producing large new editions every year.[51] Handwritten manuscripts were obviously expensive, but it is difficult to make any generalization for lack of standards. The supply of textbooks was always small, which contributed to their high cost. Copies quickly became tattered and illegible, and the making of new ones was a laborious task. In the days of book scarcity and high prices, the financial limitations of students prevented their acquisition of these luxuries. For this and other reasons the principal work of the university dealers during the

thirteenth century and the first part of the fourteenth was not
the selling, but the renting of books. [52]   A law framed in
1342 in Paris, which codified existing practices, compelled
all public booksellers to keep books to lend on rental.   The
rate of charge was fixed by the university and the students
borrowing the books were permitted to transcribe them if
they chose to do so. [53] The loaning of manuscripts to students for their own transcribing formed an important portion
of the manuscript business. [54]

　　The medieval universities developed a method of multiplication of their textbooks which, while not comparable to
the quantity production and circulation in Paris, was as well
developed as it was time-consuming.   The basis of this system was the "stationarius," whose name derived from the
Latin word statio, which in medieval Europe referred to the
workshop of a scribe.   The stationarius was definitely a
member of the university organization and operated under
rules and regulations first introduced at the University of
Bologna in Italy and further developed and adjusted at the
Sorbonne in Paris.   This term, which first appears in Paris
after the middle of the thirteenth century, indicates a change
in the method of work of the university scribes compared with
those earlier scribes or copyists who had been ready to do
work in one place or another as opportunity presented itself. [55]
Later the term was used to designate a master scribe who
directed the work of a bureau of copyists.   Later still, just
prior to the advent of printing, the stationarius, now also
called "stationarius librorum," possessed a complete bookmaking establishment where illuminators, binders, and other artisans were employed in addition to the copyists.   At this
stage, the stationarius became the equivalent of the printer-
publisher of a later generation. [56] The special responsibility
of the stationarii was to keep in stock a sufficient number of
authorized and verified transcripts or copies of the books ordered or recommended in the educational courses of the university, and to rent these to the students or to the instructors at rates prescribed by university regulation based upon
the length of the text.   The buyers of books in a university
town could purchase only the use of the books during their
stay there.   On leaving the town, the books were to be placed
again with the stationarii for sale to others associated with
the university. [57] A student could thus either purchase a textbook, or borrow it for study, or borrow it for the purpose
of copying it himself.   The basis of all these transactions
was not an entire volume, but a loose gathering called a
"pecia." At first, the extent of these divisions must have

been more or less arbitrary, but later the number of pages or sheets to be contained in them was made a matter of specific university regulation. The pecia served as the unit of calculation for the rental charge. This practice of dividing the manuscripts into portions facilitated the manifolding and prompt distributions of the texts needed and also lessened for the students the costs of securing these texts.[58]

In order to prevent the wandering of manuscripts to other centers of learning, where their existence might create an undesirable threat to a university's valuable monopoly in the field of higher education, the stationarii were officially encouraged to buy back at good prices used copies of texts from graduating students on their leaving town, which texts would then be sold to next year's freshmen.[59] Thus a trade in second-hand books developed, providing its own opportunities for unethical practices, and this second-hand market became well known to medieval students. The stationarii were generally an important link in the book trade of their time. In Paris they belonged to the same guild as the bookbinders and illuminators.[60]

With the increase in the number of students and the expansion of the curriculum, the practice gradually grew of purchasing instead of renting the texts required, and the stationarii developed into "librarii."[61] Originally the term "librarius" meant librarian, and the bookdealers who devoted themselves to keeping collections of manuscripts in the earlier years of the manuscript period did in fact fill the role of librarians rather than that of booksellers. As late as the fourteenth century, the French word librairie was used to refer to a library or a collection of books.[62] The librarii were ready to rent out their manuscripts for a consideration or to permit customers to consult the texts without taking them from the shop. The practice of making from their original stock of texts authenticated copies for general sale was a matter of rather slow development. Not until after the introduction of printing and the development of the bookshop did the term "librairie" come to denote a collection of books held for sale.[63]

For a number of years there was practically no selling of books in connection with the university work of production in Paris, and consequently, while the control of the university was exercised over the entire book trade, the authorities were more concerned about those divisions relating to the production of books.[64]

The second purpose for the existence of the book trade was to provide correct and complete texts of the prescribed works. Since the texts recommended for the work of the university belonged of necessity to the class of scholarship, their reproduction called for a background of scholarly knowledge on the part of the scribes and also for a detailed and careful supervision on the part of the university authorities. [65] The nature of the bookseller's business required no ordinary capabilities. The purchasing of manuscripts, the work of transcription, the preparation of materials, the illuminations, the binding--each of these operations required talent and discrimination. The bookseller was expected to be well informed on all branches of science and to have a knowledge of those subjects and works of which he produced transcripts. Moreover, the university required of the bookseller a guarantee of his wealth and testimonials of his good character; and, furthermore, he must promise to observe and submit to all the present and future laws and regulations of the university. [66] Manuscripts were not to be exposed without first being inspected. If errors were discovered, the copies were ordered to be burned or a fine was levied proportionate to their inaccuracy. [67] While this rule appears harsh and stringent, it is understandable when it is recalled that education was dependent upon the text itself and that the student was dependent upon the scribe for the fidelity of the copies. Since each handwritten manuscript was a separate unit, supervision was necessarily detailed, and the completeness and correctness of each individual copy had to be verified. It was essential that these copies should be entrusted to dependable persons in order that there should be no risk of inaccuracies in the texts themselves or of any unnecessary increase in the costs to masters or students in the purchase or rental of manuscripts. On the basis of these requirements, the university authorities held that it was their responsibility to supervise those operations by which university texts were prepared and circulated. From the beginning of its history, therefore, the University of Paris asserted its right to control the book trade of the city. [68] With this control came as an effect the privileges granted to the dealers as members of the university body, but there seems to be no evidence that the booksellers enjoyed these privileges before 1250. [69] Being under the direct control of the university authorities also gave the bookdealers control of a practical monopoly of the business of producing books. While this monopoly of supplying textbooks whether through sale or rental must have been an important material advantage, it involved certain disadvantages. [70]

Prior to the middle of the thirteenth century, the book trade, although it owed its origin to the university, had not yet been brought thoroughly under university control. With the intent of providing alike for the literary needs of all classes and degrees, the University of Paris framed a code of laws and regulations; and to effect this, it obtained royal sanction which put the book trade entirely under its protection. From the university authorities the book trade received its statutes, regulations, and its licenses. The university seems to have taken no action until 1275, when it passed the first regulation. [71] These first statutes give detailed regulations concerning the book trade. They specify what texts and what number of copies of each text the licensed booksellers should keep in stock. They also give a schedule, as was done in Bologna and Padua, of the prices at which the loans and sales should be made. In contrast to Bologna and Padua, however, it seems that in accordance with Parisian methods an earlier development took place in the practice of making an absolute sale of the required texts. The trade in the materials used in the manifolding of books was also strictly supervised. [72] The university's right to license was one method of control.

Booksellers possessing a university license were called "libraires jurés." These licensed booksellers were located in the Latin Quarter, together with the sellers of parchment, the illuminators, the scribes, the binders and others who also carried university licenses and were under university supervision. [73] In addition to the licensed booksellers, there were in Paris certain unlicensed dealers who began to compete with them. The locality occupied by these unlicensed dealers, who were known as book pedlars, was the Ile de la Cité near the precincts of Notre Dame Cathedral. [74] Although these pedlars enjoyed no university privileges, their business was subjected to the supervision of the university authorities. An ordinance of Charles VI, dated 1411, prohibited pedlars, hucksters, and other unlicensed dealers from taking part in the selling of manuscripts. The edict specified that the carrying on of the book business by "ignorant and irresponsible dealers" not only caused injury to the licensed bookdealers, but was a wrong upon the public in that it furthered the circulation of incorrect, incomplete, and fraudulent manuscripts. Various conflicts inevitably arose between the licensed and the unlicensed dealers. [75] Booksellers were further restricted in the economy of their trade by a rule which forbade any one of them to dispose of his entire stock of books without the consent of the university.

The bookseller was also not permitted to purchase books
without university approval lest they should be of an immoral
or heretical tendency.   Furthermore, he was specifically forbidden to buy any books from students without the permission
of the rector. [76] This rule, among others, derived from the
third purpose for the existence of the book trade: to protect
members of the university from the contamination of heretical writings or of heretical commentaries on books of accepted orthodoxy.

        Behind the university was the Church.   At the end of
the thirteenth century and into the fourteenth, the University
of Paris was the most renowned teaching center of all Christendom, particularly in theology.   This fame and the emphasis upon theology affected the volume of book production, the
need for censorship, and the growth of the city of Paris.

        In the discussion on Abelard it was noted that through
his influence "the theological school of Paris became the
seminary of Christian Europe, " and this influence continued
through the succeeding centuries.   With papal support, Paris
became the great transalpine center of orthodox theological
teaching.   Successive pontiffs cultivated friendly relations
with the University of Paris and used their influence to discourage the formation of theological faculties at other centers.
The University of Paris became known as the school where
theology was studied in its most scientific spirit, and the
decisions of its doctors were regarded as almost final. [77]
By the early fourteenth century the University of Paris was
the most important in Europe for theological studies.   Its
reputation was such that the greatest thinkers of the age had
to establish their reputation there.   The German Dominican
Albert Magnus taught there in the thirteenth century as did
the Franciscan Saint Bonaventura of Tuscany and the great
metaphysical genius Saint Thomas Aquinas.   Students came
to Paris from all over Europe. [78]   As a center of learning
Paris was unrivaled.

        The international character of education, the prestige
of the University of Paris as the center of the intellectual
life of Christendom and the theological arbiter of Europe,
the large student body and the fame of the masters, the influence of the popes: all of these factors and others also
affected the volume of book production, and book production
was in turn affected by the spirit of the times.

        Religious forces dominated, permeated, shaped the

Middle Ages. The Church provided the framework within
which Christian life and culture expressed themselves. The
ethos of society, the whole system of ideals and values that
dominated medieval culture, was permeated by these religious
forces and thus tended to control the behavior of society. A
scale of values was accepted which, although it might be re-
sented, criticized or challenged, constituted a way of life and
a standard of public opinion for medieval man.[79] Common
thoughts, common images, common words, common ideas
shaped the actions and the works of medieval society and
distinguished it from other societies. Various strands of the
heritages of thought had been collected during the Middle
Ages. What had been thought and said and done in the past,
it was believed, should be thought and said and done again.
Perhaps the most intensely felt of the things people said was
the primacy of the ideal and the spiritual and the internal
over the actual and the physical and the external. Even the
seemingly most insignificant event or activity was given a
strong religious accent. To this attitude art conformed.
Medieval man created things that provoked wonder. Miracles
happened; manuscripts glowed; shrines inspired. These
values shaped the character of the city of Paris into that of
an ecclesiastical city, flaming into full glory in the twelfth
and thirteenth centuries, finding physical expression in its
dominant structures of Notre Dame Cathedral and Sainte-
Chapelle. These religious forces shaped in a not inconsider-
able way the character of the earliest issues of the Paris
press.

   The association of the Church with the book trade was
an important one, for Paris booksellers dealt largely with
theological writings. Publishers found themselves dependent
upon the scholarly interests and the scholarly cooperation of
the clerics. Printers in sixteenth-century Paris devoted
their presses exclusively to theology and to the classics.
The task of producing books for scholarly and critical readers was increased by the exactions of ecclesiastical censorship as well as other severe rules and regulations. Printing became an instrument of spiritual and intellectual development and theological and scientific discourse, but the earliest
reaction, which persisted for centuries, was one of opposition
by university, Church and government to its use in giving wide
publicity to certain ideas and information. The system of
censorship, ecclesiastical and political, dates in substance
from that great force of the sixteenth century, the Reformation.[80]

The contention of the University of Paris to control
the book trade as a part of the work of higher education,
while sharply attacked and undermined after the middle of
the seventeenth century, was not formally abandoned until
the beginning of the eighteenth. For six centuries the book
trade of Paris, the makers and sellers of books either handwritten or printed, had to contend with the regulations and
restrictions of a varying series of authorities: the rectors
of the University of Paris, the theologians of the Sorbonne,
the lawyers of the Parlement of Paris, the chancellors of
the Crown, the kings themselves, the influence of the Church
and the authority of the Crown being channeled through the
university machinery. All had taken a part in the task of
regulating the trade in books. [81] The various regulations,
while possibly required in connection with the general interests of the university to implement the purpose of the book
trade, to prevent any unwarranted increase in the market
price or selling value of manuscripts, or the "cornering of
the market" by the booksellers in connection with texts which
might be in demand, or the materials used in their production, were exacting. [82] University control meant censorship,
restriction, supervision, regulation of prices, interference
with trade facilities, and various other conditions which seriously impeded the natural development of the book trade,
not to mention placing obstacles in the way of the intellectual
development of the lay community.

    As an instrument of publishing, printing had to fight
its way. The printing industry inherited with the manuscript
publishing tradition all of its privileges and its controls.
Both were intensified by the advent of printing. At first the
printers were left free to reproduce such works as they
themselves might select. No claim had yet been made for
exclusive ownership in or control of literary productions,
and no censorship supervision had been established on the
part of the government. [83] The marketing of books was giv-
en a powerful stimulus with the introduction of printing, and
the kings of France, impressed with the possibilities of this
new method of reproduction, recognized that it was to their
advantage and in the interests of the realm to free books,
printed or written, from customs or importation charges or
other taxes and tolls. [84] This situation continued during the
reign of Louis XII, and in an edict issued in 1513 the king
confirmed and extended the privileges which had previously
been granted to the booksellers as officials of the University
of Paris. [85] By the end of the fifteenth century and into the

early decades of the sixteenth the protection of the kings and
the university had established the book business in the national economy as a favored infant industry.[86] Francis I,
who ruled from 1515 to 1547 and prided himself on his taste
for literature and showed much regard for the scholarly publishers and editors, was interested in fostering both printing
and bookselling at the beginning of his reign. The introduction and spread of Protestantism and pressure from the Sorbonne, however, soon forced him to pass restrictions on the
products of the press.[87] Censorship control over the moral
character and orthodoxy of the works printed was insisted
upon more strenuously than ever by the theological faculty
of the Sorbonne, behind whom stood the Church of Rome, as
the importance of the influence upon public opinion of the
widely distributed printed volumes began to be realized. The
authority of the university, expressed through the theological
faculty, was from the beginning of the Reformation persistent
in its exercise of a rigorous censorship which restricted
nearly all classes of publishing undertakings.[88] The spirit
of the time was stronger than any one king, and the persis-
tency of the Church proved too strong to be offset by the
friendly interest and the liberal policies of the Crown. The
ecclesiastical control of the printing press became before
1540 an established and obstructive fact.

The theological faculty of the Sorbonne had provoked
a serious conflict, it will be recalled, when the mendicant
friars, in disregard of academic practice, had presented for
divinity degrees friars who had not followed an arts course,
a procedure bitterly opposed by the secular masters who insisted that the arts course was indispensable. With the conflict settled in their favor by the pope, the mendicants were
allowed to occupy university chairs, thus at the same time
increasing the pope's influence in the affairs of the Sorbonne.
It followed, then, that the faculty of the Sorbonne was gradually filled by doctors who, although they had attained a reputation for orthodoxy, did not possess the necessary liberal
arts qualifications.[89] As theological censors, the faculty
members were irate at the assumption by the publisher,
acting as his own editor, of the right to correct Scripture
texts and to add marginal commentaries. They were also
indignant at the king's interference with the right of the theological faculty to exercise a censorship control over all
theological and religious publications emanating from the
French press.[90] Possessing little or no knowledge of Greek,
the Sorbonne doctors were inclined to believe that any Greek
work might contain some dangerous heresy. As a result,

some of the mendicant doctors denounced the Greek and Roman classics as pagan and harbored suspicions of previously accepted versions, maintaining that "a knowledge of the Greek and Hebrew languages would operate to the destruction of all religion."[91] The faculty of theology at the Sorbonne published lists of prohibited books, which are the earliest among the numerous indices librorum prohibitorum. Infringements of the restrictions imposed were punishable by death. Many a French printer with inclinations toward the new religion met his fate in this way, two of whom were Antoine Augereau, printer and punch cutter, who was hanged and burned at Paris in 1534, and Étienne Dolet, a printer who in 1546 had been charged with blasphemy, sedition, and the selling of prohibited books, for which he too was committed to the flames.[92]

Supervision of books was of great concern not only to the prelates or the popes, but also to the government. At about this same time, the acts of the Paris Parlement gradually extended censorship to medical, astrological, legal, and literary books, as well as to those intended for elementary education. For the enforcement of these controls a series of edicts was issued under Henry II and his successors, ranging from 1549 to 1561. Under the reign of Charles IX, censorship became not only religious but political with the Order of 1563, confirmed in 1566, which reserved for the chancellor of the king alone the right to grant an "approbation" or "privilege" to the printer or bookseller.[93] As late as 1618, in the reign of Charles IX, the master printers were obliged to hold certificates from the rector and the university to the effect that they were skilled in the art of printing and that they possessed full knowledge of Latin and Greek.[94] The dividing line in the history of the French book trade is marked by the date, June 16, 1618. Before this, the book trade was an irregular organization, part free, part regulated, a division of the university yet subject to preliminary efforts to bring it closer to the civil government. After this date a new corporation, the Syndical and Royal Chamber of Booksellers, Printers, and Binders of Paris, came into being with a complete monopoly on the business and with the legal power to carry out the regulations of the royal government.[95] This did not mean freedom from controls, however, for control of the publishing effort in France was more or less thorough until the revolutionary copyright law of 1793 which freed publishing and printing from all existing monopolies. This too was short-lived, ending with Napoleon's First Empire, and was not restored until the declaration of the republic in 1870.[96]

Some of the regulations were instituted to settle the relationship between employer and employee. Labor troubles reached a crisis in 1539 with a strike at Paris, and an even more serious one at Lyons. The conditions under which the journeymen worked were bad, and the hours of labor incredibly long, even after a settlement was reached.[97]

Johnson points out that it was neither censorship nor labor troubles which was responsible for the great falling off in both the quality and the quantity of books produced in France toward the close of the sixteenth century, but that the chief cause was the wars of religion which began in 1562.[98] The wars of religion provided setbacks to the progress of printing in France. Many Huguenot Protestant printers emigrated to Switzerland, England and the Low Countries, and the center of printing activity moved to the Low Countries.[99]

It is surprising, wrote Putnam, that the printer-publishers of Paris should have been able to do so much to make Paris a literary and a publishing center in the face of the long series of difficulties, difficulties more serious than those with which any publishers in the world outside of Rome had to contend.[100] Some of this success may be attributed to the manuscript heritage. The manuscript publishing tradition which the printing industry inherited provided a firm foundation for the new industry. Although based upon this well-established foundation, the printing method faced technical problems resulting from the need to adapt and adjust the existing practices to the new technology. The steps in the actual production of the earliest printed books were not very different in essence from those involved in manuscript preparation: after the scribe had finished copying, his work was proofread by a second person; the sheets were sent to a rubricator who inserted titles, headlines, chapter and other initials; if the manuscript was to be illustrated, the sheets were then sent to the illuminator; after which the volume was ready to be bound. One time-saving difference was that with the products of the printing press, these and other related tasks had to be performed only once for an edition of many hundreds.[101] The printing production method, although it had evolved from the manuscript method, presented its own challenges and requirements. The business carried on by the early printers differed materially from the business of their predecessors and from that of their successors. These early printers had the responsibility of initiating and of shaping the

literary undertakings of the time.   In addition to adapting the
machinery of bookmaking to new uses or creating anew where
necessary, dependable copies of works best suited to the
needs of the first buyers of printed books had to be selected
and edited and the type-setting for them supervised.   They
had to supply capital; take necessary risks; provide equipment, supplies, labor.   Steps had to be taken for securing
a legal status for the new class of property being brought
into existence.   In the absence of precedents, it became
necessary to convince princes, ministers, councils, parlia-
ments to establish and defend property rights for the producers; after which it was still necessary to conciliate the
Church. 102   With the requirements came the men.   Society
had the exceptional individuals necessary to develop the full
scope and usefulness of the art of printing.   The producers
who accepted the challenges and succeeded in creating a publishing business, and in producing for their own times and
for posterity long lists of costly and scholarly editions of
the great literature of their world, were men of achievement.
These were the printer-publishers. 103

       Two exceptional individuals of this early period were
Henry Estienne, who started the revolution in typography,
and Simon de Colines, who widened the precedents and added
innovations of his own.   Henry Estienne (d. 1520) was the
founder of the distinguished family of scholarly printers, the
above-mentioned house of Estienne, latinized as Stephanus.
The famous Estienne family, whose publishing business was
to continue for nearly a century and a half, ranked with the
great publishers and scholars of the time.   Henry Estienne
carried on his work under difficulties commercial, literary,
theological, political.   The classics were the chief products
of his press, which show his skill in combining the best features of French and Italian typography.   After his first book,
which was dated 1504, he published in all about a hundred
separate works, all of which, with hardly an exception,
were in Latin.   Henry Estienne assumed personal responsibility for the typographical accuracy of his texts.   He regarded his publishing imprint as a guarantee of trustworthy
work, and every typographical error as a stain upon his
character as a publisher.   His works were considered heretical by the doctors of the Sorbonne and, in spite of the
special interference of Francis I, by whom his merits were
held in high esteem, he was expelled from the University of
Paris. 104

       The successors of Henry Estienne were Simon de

Colines, an associate, who married his widow, and Robert Estienne, his son. Colines and Robert Estienne may be called the first French Renaissance printers.[105] These two were the first of the Paris printers to adopt the italic type. They published the Greek and Latin classics at prices suitable for students, adopted the small format first utilized by Aldus Manutius in Venice, and produced a reformed roman type which was to be the standard European type for two centuries. Although Colines introduced to Paris the best features of the Aldine Press, he was not an imitator, as a comparison of the two reveals. Colines' books show a tendency to variety and a workmanlike yet delicate execution, McMurtrie points out, that is distinctly French in tone.[106] The most important of the works of contemporary writers which bore Colines' imprint was an edition of the Colloquies of Erasmus. This work was banned by the Sorbonne censor, but before it was withdrawn from the market no less than twenty-four thousand copies were printed. The editions of Colines included a very full list of the leading Latin authors, with special attention given to Cicero.[107] The chief prestige associated with the work of Colines came from his beautiful editions of works in Greek. Colines was printing from 1520 until 1546, and is credited with seven hundred and thirty-four books.[108] Henry Estienne and Simon de Colines are worthy representatives of the scholarly pioneers who devoted themselves to the new art of printing until it could be carried on as a business enterprise without the necessity of exceptional individuals for its direction.[109]

The work of the early printer-publishers furthered the development of scholarly publishing and the production of scholarly books, as lists of the works published by their presses indicate. Since the literature best suited to the first buyers of books toward which the efforts of the printer-publishers were directed consisted of works prepared to meet the requirements of the scholars of the day, in addition to producing editions of the Scriptures, their choice of books was influenced to a great extent by the fact that the control of the first French presses rested with the University of Paris. These first issues were, consequently, largely restricted to editions of the classics or to works of law and medicine belonging to the official lists of the university texts.[110] It was for this class of publications that the publishers had to secure the first liberties in the form of protections and privileges from the rulers. The liberties granted to the printers by the kings early in the sixteenth century helped to foster the great advance of French typog-

raphy. Type design was one of the great French contributions
to the art of printing. [111] The Italian campaigns of Francis
I about 1520 had brought to Paris a realization of the highest
ideals of Renaissance scholarship, which influenced both type
design and illustration. By 1530 in Paris the leading printers
had created styles of beauty which have inspired the best
book designers of the last three hundred years. [112] The most
important designer of types of the sixteenth century was
Claude Garamond, since his models of roman, italic, and
Greek types, either in their pure form or as adapted by subsequent cutters, dominated type design until the late eighteenth century and are highly successful in modern revivals. [113]
Colines made successful use of roman type in books while
more conservative printers still employed the ornate black
letter of the Gothic period. Robert Estienne concerned himself with the purity of his texts. Geoffrey Tory, as a reactionary, had the greatest influence on book illustration: he
modeled his woodcuts in pure outline without any form of
shading. As a theorizer, wrote Bland, Tory goes right back
to the schoolmen of the Middle Ages, an example being the
way he makes the letters of the alphabet stand for moral
qualities. [114] One of Tory's first theories of typography was
entitled Champfleury, published in 1529. [115] With the work
of these men the French Renaissance style had arrived. In
sharp contrast to the French book of the fifteenth century
with its vigor and variety, the new style displayed, as
McMurtrie described it, "a chaste simplicity, a classical
restraint, and a delicate refinement which is typically renaissance in spirit. "[116]

With the distinctly French Renaissance style of book
production came a success so great that Paris rapidly became the leading city in Europe in all the arts of the book.
"It is hardly possible, " Johnson observed, "to open a Paris
book of the period which is not of first-rate quality. "[117]
Like their predecessors, these early printer-publishers
passed on to posterity a rich publishing tradition, for the
period of the first half of the sixteenth century in Paris was
styled the "golden age of typography. "[118] At this time Paris
was favorably situated to have a leading part in any movement in typography, McMurtrie observed. [119] Paris was
probably the largest and most important city in Europe; it
was far enough removed to escape the violence of the religious controversy that was tearing apart the cities to the
north, yet close enough to share the intellectual excitement
that the conflict engendered; it was fortunate in having successive kings who were patrons of both letters and typography;

it was the seat of a university which, although extremely
conservative and in a state of decline, was still the largest
and most important institution of learning in Europe.[120] It
was this combination of material prosperity and intellectual
stimulation, McMurtrie concluded, that made the first sixty
years in Paris the golden age of typography.[121]

It might have been expected that Paris, with all its
fame and its renown as the most important center for literary production during the manuscript period and as the
place where scholars came to look for material, would have
been among the first cities to which the art of printing would
spread after its invention in Mainz about 1450, but this did
not happen until about twenty years later. After printing
was introduced into Paris in response to a growing demand,
the normal operation of the printing industry as a private
enterprise was hampered by the strict regulations and censorship, which contributed to the eventual exodus of printers
and the decline of the printing industry in Paris. Fust and
Schoeffer, from Mainz, introduced the printed book to Paris.
Beginning as early as the 1460s, they visited Paris repeated-
ly with their productions and maintained a permanent agent
there. The demand for printed books had begun.[122] It increased rapidly after the introduction of printing into Paris,
and before the close of the fifteenth century the trade in
books far exceeded that of any city in Europe. Much of this
demand, however, was supplied, in addition to the work of
the presses of Mainz, from those of Strassburg, Venice,
Milan, Cologne, and Bruges.[123] The printing press had been
in use in France for three-quarters of a century and the demand for books had still been restricted in large part to the
scholarly circles of the universities and of the educated ecclesiastics.[124] Being still a section of the university, the
printing industry was not yet being operated as a private enterprise, even though with the protection of the Crown and
the university it had become established as a favored infant
industry in the national economy.[125] The granting of privileges and favors indicates a growth of trade consciousness
and the rapid rise of the printer to publishing eminence.
However, although only forty years after the introduction of
printing there were already established in Paris over fifty
printing concerns, the various regulations interfered not a
little with any natural development of the printed book trade,
affecting both the demand and the supply of books.[126] The
demand from university and ecclesiastical centers for the
editions of the Scriptures and for all theological works was
impeded materially by the adverse influence of the theologians

of the Sorbonne, while the sale of Bibles, Putnam declared, was absolutely blocked for several long periods.[127] The general effect of regulations controlling prices and profits in supplying students with books was to discourage private initiative. Not until some time after the introduction of printing did the importance and prospect of profit outside of the university limits and freedom from university regulations appear to be sufficiently worthwhile for certain of the more enterprising of the printers to give up their privileges and their trade in textbooks and establish themselves as independent dealers.[128]

While the profit motive was one force which contributed to placing the printing industry into a more competitive position in the French economy, the widening of the reading public to include those outside the circles of instructors and students also contributed by creating a popular demand for books. In sharp contrast to the earlier products of the Mainz press, which belonged in no way to the university curriculum but were addressed directly to the common people, book production for popular circulation in France began with the Reformation.[129]

The Reformation, turning as it did upon intellectual issues such as the history of the Church and the exegesis of the Scriptures and of the writings of the Church Fathers, developed much activity among the intellectuals throughout Europe, but all the writings of the Protestants were classed as heretical.[130] The increasingly bitter strife of the theologians and the controversies of the scholars which followed had the effect on the common people of arousing them into a state of ferment. This ferment extended the range of the reading public by bringing about a development in intellectual activities and literary interests, causing many to read who had never read before and those who did know how, to read more.[131] With the eager popular demand for instruction and information came a correspondingly intensified severity in the system of censorship. No censorship, however, could restrain the growing activity of the press, an activity awakened by this increase in popular demand. The men whose work it was to produce for the public asked to be let alone, but they asked in vain.[132]

Printing was a capitalistic industry from the start, requiring a large initial outlay for the necessary equipment, supplies and inventories. A certain amount of capital as well as a wide range of literary information and scholarly

training was, therefore, needed. With the supremacy of
Catholic orthodoxy in France, it was not possible to carry
on with any sufficient assurance as to the future a publishing
business which involved taking calculated risks in the planning of large undertakings. The leading publishers and their
editorial associates who were investing their time and their
capital came to the conclusion that the advantages of Paris
as a literary and commercial center were not sufficient to
offset the continued annoyances they were receiving. Paris
publishers began to migrate. [133] The publishing business of
England, of Switzerland and the Low Countries received
after the beginning of the Reformation an exceptional impetus
and development through the migration of Paris publishers
and the transfer of the literary undertakings of French
scholars. In England it is estimated that from 1476 to 1536,
two-thirds of all printers, binders, and stationers were
aliens. [134] The Swiss capital of Geneva in particular presented special advantages for the publishing business in the
middle years of the sixteenth century, and as a result it became the most important center for the production of the
controversial literature of the Protestants. [135] It was to
Geneva that Robert Estienne removed his printing concern in
1552 after his interest in Biblical texts and his Protestant
tendencies made him appear suspect to the censors of the
Sorbonne and after the death of his patron, Francis I, in
1547. [136] The Geneva house of Estienne was continued by
the second Henry Estienne, an even more famous scholar
and editor of Greek texts than his father. French restrictions also had a beneficial effect upon the Low Countries,
which became the center of printing activity after the middle
of the sixteenth century, particularly the city of Antwerp,
where Christophe Plantin, who fled from Paris to escape religious persecution in 1548, established the printing concern
which was to secure high distinction as one of the strongest
in Europe with its foundry, bindery, and bookshop. [137] After
1560, Paris lost its supremacy as a book production center.

Volume of Production

     Restricted though they were, the book merchants, nev-
ertheless, transacted an extensive trade. The middle years
of the sixteenth century in particular were a period of great
activity for the printing press at Paris, a period notable
both for the high standard of workmanship and for the quantity of books produced. During this period the growth of the
publishing industry increased to the extent that it contributed

to the physical expansion of the city of Paris.   Since actual
statistics on the number of books produced in the sixteenth
century in Paris are not available, two other criteria have
been selected which reflect this growth: the number of persons engaged in the publishing industry, and the growth of
the university library.

Scholars have used various categories in collecting
data on the publishing industry.   A scholar named Levasseur
estimated that in the sixteenth century there were eight hundred printers, dealers, and binders in Paris.[138]   Data given
in a semiofficial catalog of members of the Paris book trade
issued by Augustin Martin Lottin in 1789 show that in the
sixteenth century a total of six hundred and thirty-five individuals were received as master printers and booksellers,
as compared to eighty for the period between 1470 and
1499.[139]   Pottinger is confident that the work of the great
bibliographer Philippe Renouard is reliable.   Renouard's
work was first published in 1898, and after many years of
further investigation, a complete revision was published in
a series of articles dating from 1922 to 1934.   Renouard
shows that a total of eighteen hundred and forty, including
printers, booksellers, typefounders, proofreaders and others
in the trade, were at work in Paris in the sixteenth century.
Of this total, one hundred and three had begun in the fifteenth
century and carried over into the sixteenth.[140]   For the entire kingdom, Pottinger quotes Montchrétien as reporting to
Louis XIII in 1615:   "I can say without exaggeration that
there are fifty thousand persons in your kingdom who are
engaged in printing and bookselling and who have no other
sources of income."[141]   While there appears to be a wide
divergence, some of this may be attributed to the kinds of
data used.   Compared to Renouard's figure, Levasseur's
total included "dealers and binders," which may or may not
have been included in Renouard's miscellaneous category,
"and others in the trade," while Lottin listed masters only.
Lottin shows an increase of five hundred and fifty-five
masters in the sixteenth century over the fifteenth, while
Renouard shows an increase in the book-producing population
of seventeen hundred and thirty-seven in the sixteenth century over the fifteenth.   Although Pottinger doubts the credi-
bility of the Montchrétien report, it does reflect a flourishing
state of the book trade and, since Paris was the leading
center of book production in France in the sixteenth century,
it may be assumed that a large number of these workers
were located in Paris.   After making due allowance for the
variance, the data nevertheless show a substantial increase

in the sixteenth century over the fifteenth in the number of
people engaged in the publishing industry.

Since the focus of the discussion on Paris is upon its
role as a university city, the development of the university
library is a meaningful index of the growth of the publishing
industry. The discussion examines this growth as it was
reflected in the collections, the organization of the library,
and the architectural expansion of the library.

At Paris the earliest definite information regarding a
library comes with the foundation of the college of the Sorbonne in 1257. The library of the Sorbonne had its origin
with the generosity of Robert de Sorbon who, as a part of
his endowment, gave his own personal library of about sixty-
seven volumes to the school, [142] along with money for its
upkeep. [143] Books were an essential part of the Sorbonne's
life, and the library grew rapidly after its inception. Addi-
tions to the collection came from the generosity of friends
and from grateful students and professors, as shown in a
list of nearly two hundred benefactors from the middle of
the thirteenth to the end of the fifteenth century. [144] The
collection was further augmented by numerous works produced at the expense of the university, from books left as
pledges in payment of debts, from authors who gave copies
of their works, through exchanges, and through the purchase
of new books. [145]

Four catalogs are known to have been made of the
Sorbonne collection, in 1289, 1290, 1321, and 1338, all of
which have been published. By 1289 the collection numbered
one thousand and seventeen titles, of which only four were
in French and the remainder in Latin. According to this
catalog, the books were arranged in ten major divisions including theology, medicine, law, and the seven subjects of
the trivium and quadrivium. [146] By this date the library
was formally organized. With a collection of this size, a
division into two parts, a main library and a circulating department, was considered practical. The reference works
and the best manuscripts were chained to desks in fixed locations in the main library, while the small circulating library contained duplicates and books rarely used. The books
in the college chapel were considered part of the first section. [147] By 1338 the catalog showed that the collection had
increased to seventeen hundred and twenty-two volumes, and
the catalog itself was divided into three parts--the small library, the large library, and an analysis of the contents of

these books. The books were arranged under fifty-nine sub-jects.[148]

By the fourteenth century the University of Paris num-bered forty colleges which had spread to the left bank, as discussed above, and from the fourteenth to the beginning of the sixteenth century, the number of colleges had increased to about seventy. The "university" library, as the term is understood today, did not exist until the college system had developed.[149] The collections in these colleges were housed in rooms over arcades or in open corridors, and the book-desks were placed between the windows so the light could fall directly on the reading shelf. In these "libraries, " in order to meet the challenge of the printing press, reading rooms were at first made larger with added tiers of books and gal-leries.[150] The sixteenth century saw the development of bookstalls or carrels where tall bookcases held four to six shelves of books in addition to the slanted desk or reading shelf beneath. This system held many more books in the same space, and as the printed book replaced the manuscript, it completely supplanted the older desks.[151] Limits of ex-pansion for a single gallery were soon reached, and some method had to be devised for separating the public in read-ing rooms from the room for storing books. To meet this need, the separate library building came into existence. At the University of Paris approval for the erection of a sepa-rate library building was voted in 1481.[152]

The expansion of the book collection at the University of Paris, which had originated with a single collection of sixty-seven volumes, expanding to individual college libraries, then to a separate library building, thus presents an example of the increase in volume book production in lieu of actual statistics.

In the sixteenth century the University of Paris, though the largest in Europe, declined steadily both in num-bers and in learning, to which state various causes contrib-uted: the theological dissensions, the extreme conservatism of the academic authorities, involvement in the religious con-flicts of the time, and severe reduction of its resources by the wars of religion.[153] The first and brighter half of the sixteenth century in France was followed by a darker half during which the country was in flames. While the Univer-sity of Paris was already in a state of decline, the complex economic and social problems had their effect upon the pub-lishing industry in Paris in the second half of the century.

Printing, a formidable weapon in the wars of religion, was driven underground. Until about 1560, book illustration had maintained its best artistic traditions, developing styles of its own. The banning of controversial literature, however, succeeded in discouraging book illustration since forbidden texts had to be printed surreptitiously, cheaply, and quickly.[154] Both the quality and the quantity of books published in Paris declined in the second half of the sixteenth century, and the lead in publishing was taken over by Antwerp.[155] The golden age of the medieval university and of the medieval publishing industry of Paris had passed, but both were to revive and to endure in a new era.

Notes

1. Fleming, op. cit., p. 258.

2. David M. Robb and J. J. Garrison, Art in the Western World (third edition; New York: Harper and Brothers, 1953), p. 611.

3. Gombrich, op. cit., p. 159.

4. Millard Meiss, "Preface," The Très Riches Heures of Jean, Duke of Berry, op. cit., pp. 7-8.

5. Gombrich, op. cit., p. 159.

6. Meiss, op. cit., p. 10.

7. Gombrich, op. cit., p. 158.

8. Meiss, op. cit., p. 10.

9. Fleming, op. cit., p. 228.

10. Singer, op. cit., p. 121.

11. Ibid.

12. Ibid.

13. Edith Simon and others, The Reformation (Great Ages of Man Series. New York: Time Incorporated, 1966), p. 165.

14. Singer, op. cit., p. 121.

15. Howard Woodrow Winger, "Book," Encyclopaedia Britan-
     nica (1964 ed.), III, 924.

16. Ibid.

17. Ibid., Plate III.

18. Margaret Aston, The Fifteenth Century (New York:
     Harcourt, Brace and World, Inc., 1968), p. 71.

19. Douglas C. McMurtrie, The Book (third revised edi-
     tion; New York: Oxford University Press, 1943),
     p. 188.

20. Denys Hay, "Fiat Lux," Printing and the Mind of Man,
     John Carter and others, editors (New York: Holt,
     Rinehart and Winston, 1967), p. xix.

21. McLuhan, op. cit., p. 111.

22. Aston, op. cit., p. 69.

23. Hay, op. cit., p. xxiv.

24. Clark, op. cit., p. 56.

25. Winger, op. cit., p. 926.

26. Simon and others, op. cit., p. 165.

27. Hay, op. cit., p. xxi.

28. Clark, op. cit., p. 59.

29. Hay, op. cit., p. xxx.

30. McLuhan, op. cit., p. 111.

31. Hay, op. cit., p. xxx.

32. Philip Hofer, "The Illustration of Books," A History of
     the Printed Book, Lawrence C. Wroth, editor (New
     York: The Limited Editions Club, 1938), p. 395.

33. Powicke, op. cit., p. 160.

34. William Miller, "Publishing," Encyclopaedia Britannica (1964 ed.), XVIII, 749.

35. Edith Rothe, Mediaeval Book Illumination in Europe (New York: W. W. Norton and Company, Inc., 1968), pp. 14-15.

36. Ibid., pp. 18-19.

37. Ibid., p. 15.

38. David T. Pottinger, The French Book Trade in the Ancien Regime: 1500-1791 (Cambridge, Mass.: Harvard University Press, 1958), p. 114.

39. Putnam, op. cit., I, 199-200.

40. Pottinger, op. cit., p. 114.

41. Putnam, op. cit., I, 201.

42. Ibid., p. 204.

43. Hunt, op. cit., p. 200.

44. Hay, op. cit., p. xviii.

45. McLuhan, op. cit., p. 95.

46. Thompson, op. cit., p. 258.

47. Powicke, op. cit., p. 160.

48. Hellmut Lehmann-Haupt, Peter Schoeffer of Gernsheim and Mainz (New York: The Printing House of Leo Hart, 1950), p. 90.

49. Winger, op. cit., p. 926.

50. Morrall, op. cit., p. 134.

51. Miller, op. cit., p. 749.

52. Putnam, op. cit., I, 204.

53. F. Somner Merryweather, Bibliomania in the Middle Ages (London: The Woodstock Press, 1933), p. 60.

54. Putnam, op. cit., I, 194.

55. Ibid., pp. 184-85.

56. Ibid., p. 205.

57. Ibid., p. 185.

58. Ibid., p. 186.

59. Lehmann-Haupt, op. cit., p. 14.

60. Ibid.

61. Putnam, op. cit., I, 189.

62. Ibid.

63. Ibid., pp. 189-90.

64. Ibid., p. 201.

65. Ibid., p. 200.

66. Merryweather, op. cit., p. 58.

67. Ibid., p. 59.

68. Putnam, op. cit., I, 200.

69. Ibid., p. 257.

70. Ibid., p. 204.

71. Pottinger, op. cit., p. 115.

72. Putnam, op. cit., I, 264.

73. Ibid., p. 217.

74. Ibid., p. 260.

75. Ibid., p. 264.

76. Merryweather, op. cit., p. 59.

77. "Universities," op. cit., p. 864.

78. Putnam, op. cit., I, 261.

79. Reinhardt, op. cit., pp. 131-32.

80. Putnam, op. cit., II, 27.

81. Ibid., I, 214-15.

82. Ibid., p. 260.

83. Ibid., II, 6.

84. Ibid., I, 203.

85. Ibid., II, 6.

86. Pottinger, op. cit., p. 117.

87. Ibid., pp. 117-18.

88. Putnam, op. cit., II, 29.

89. McMurtrie, op. cit., p. 330.

90. Putnam, op. cit., II, 38-39.

91. McMurtrie, op. cit., p. 331.

92. A. F. Johnson, "The Sixteenth Century," A History
     of the Printed Book, op. cit., p. 144.

93. Charles Mortet, "France," Printing: A Short History
     of the Art, R. A. Peddie, editor (London: Grafton
     and Company, 1927), p. 87.

94. Putnam, op. cit., I, 206.

95. Pottinger, op. cit., p. 122.

96. Miller, op. cit., p. 750.

97. Johnson, op. cit., p. 144.

98. Ibid.

99. Miller, op. cit., p. 501.

100. Putnam, op. cit., I, 215.

101. Miller, op. cit., p. 749.

102. Putnam, op. cit., II, 15-16.

103. Ibid., p. 17.

104. Ibid., pp. 18-19.

105. Johnson, op. cit., p. 135.

106. McMurtrie, op. cit., p. 333.

107. Putnam, op. cit., II, 21-22.

108. Johnson, op. cit., p. 135.

109. Putnam, op. cit., II, 17.

110. Ibid., I, 363.

111. "Printing, " Encyclopaedia Britannica (1964 ed.), XVIII, 501.

112. David Bland, A History of Book Illustration (Berkeley, California: University of California Press, 1969), p. 170.

113. Johnson, op. cit., p. 137.

114. Bland, op. cit., p. 170.

115. Ibid.

116. McMurtrie, op. cit., p. 347.

117. Johnson, op. cit., p. 141.

118. McMurtrie, op. cit., p. 328.

119. Ibid., p. 327.

120. Ibid., pp. 327-28.

121. Ibid., p. 328.

122. Konrad Haebler, The Study of Incunabula, trans. Lucy Eugenia Osborne (New York: The Grolier Club, 1933), p. 176.

123. Putnam, op. cit., II, 7.

124. Ibid., p. 27.

125. Pottinger, op. cit., p. 118.

126. Putnam, op. cit., II, 5.

127. Ibid., p. 58.

128. Ibid., I, 205.

129. Ibid., p. 363.

130. Ibid., II, 51.

131. Ibid., p. 26.

132. Ibid., p. 27.

133. Ibid., pp. 19-20.

134. Miller, op. cit., p. 750.

135. Putnam, op. cit., II, 51.

136. Ibid., p. 46.

137. "Printing," op. cit., p. 501.

138. Pottinger, op. cit., p. 112, citing Emile Levasseur, Histoire des classes ouvrières et de l'industrie en France avant 1789, 1900-1901, II, 31.

139. Ibid., p. 114, citing Augustin Martin Lottin, Catalogue chronologique des imprimeurs et libraires de Paris, 1789, p. iii.

140. Ibid., citing Philippe Renouard, Imprimeurs parisiens, libraires, fondeurs de caractères d'imprimerie à Paris 1470 jusqu'à la fin du XVIᵒ siècle.

141. Ibid., p. 112, citing Antoine de Montchrétien, Traicté

de l'oeconomie politique, Frantz Funck-Brentano, editor, 1889, p. 91.

142. Hunt, op. cit., p. 201.

143. Elmer D. Johnson, A History of Libraries in the Western World (New York: The Scarecrow Press, Inc., 1965), p. 123.

144. Thompson, op. cit., p. 438.

145. Ibid., p. 256.

146. Johnson, A History of Libraries in the Western World, op. cit., p. 123.

147. Thompson, op. cit., p. 257.

148. Ibid., p. 439.

149. Hunt, op. cit., p. 201.

150. Walter Harrington Kilham, "Library Architecture," Encyclopaedia Britannica (1964 ed.), XIV, 25.

151. Johnson, A History of Libraries in the Western World, op. cit., p. 127.

152. Thompson, op. cit., p. 439.

153. "Universities," op. cit., p. 870.

154. Hofer, op. cit., p. 401.

155. Johnson, "The Sixteenth Century," op. cit., p. 144.

Chapter 8

EXPANSION

The organic division of Paris into a congeries of cities, shaped as this division was by geographical and topographical characteristics which made the Ile de la Cité the site of the royal city and the ecclesiastical city; the right bank, the site of the mercantile city; and the left bank, the site of the university city, was complemented by another kind of division into functional precincts based upon vocation. The left bank became the professional quarter, and it was here that the achievement of the publishing industry left its characteristic imprint upon the face of the city of Paris. The names of the streets speak of this achievement, but they tell of the manuscript legacy which had been bequeathed to the printing industry. Since the present is blended with the past, the following discussion traces the expansion of the publishing industry and the mark it left upon the left bank from the time of Abelard through the sixteenth century, presenting in review within this context the effect of the geographical and topographical features upon the direction of this growth. This is followed by a discussion of the physical expansion of the city of Paris.

Expansion of the Left Bank

The hills on the left bank, although moderate in relief, approached close to the Seine, which tended to hamper the development of that area. In the time of Abelard, about 1140, the city on the Ile de la Cité was expanding outward toward either bank. The left bank was still covered with vineyards and farms. The schools, soon to be called a university, spread to this less-developed area of the city. Even after it was enclosed within the wall of Philip II Augustus, about 1209, it still remained a semirural expanse of vineyards. The left bank was also the domain of the Church, and mendicant friars had settled themselves in the less de-

sirable areas along the walls in the mid-thirteenth century.
With the growth of the University of Paris, various colleges
were added.

Through the establishment of places to study such as
convents and colleges, the left bank became at an early date
the professional quarter. To supply the shifting population
of teachers, students, and bibliophiles, publishing houses
sprang up which gathered together the specialists in book
production--the scribes, correctors, illuminators, parchmentmakers, binders, and other artisans. [1] In Paris the business of the dealers in manuscripts was carried on in booths
or shops, in various open places but very largely in the immediate vicinity of the churches, although certain booths
were also located on the bridges and near the courts of justice. An area particularly favored was the Rue Neuve Notre
Dame and the bridge Neuf Notre Dame. [2] Quays were lined
with shops of goldsmiths, watchmakers, illuminators, craftsmen, artisans who had resided first in the Ile de la Cité
near Notre Dame, moving to the left bank in the vicinity of
the university when the Sorbonne came to occupy its own
permanent quarters. [3] As the University of Paris extended
its control over the publishing industry, the licensed dealers
became separated from their unlicensed competitors. Those
booksellers with licenses were located on the left bank, now
called the Latin Quarter or the University Quarter, among
others of the book-producing population who also carried
university licenses. The unlicensed dealers occupied the
locality on the Ile de la Cité within the shadow of Notre
Dame Cathedral. [4]

The people concerned with book production, most of
whom lived in the vicinity of the university, were drawn together into streets or quarters by similar trades or occupations. [5] The names of the streets speak for themselves.
The Rue de la Parcheminerie, the street of the parchmentmakers, with its public scribes, copyists, and parchment
vendors, crosses the Rue des Enlumineurs, or street of the
illuminators, now the Rue Boutebrie. [6] Running parallel to
the Seine is the street of the woodmen, the Rue de la
Bûcherie, which was laid out across a vineyard in 1202. [7]
Nearby is the Rue du Fouarre, the street of straw on which
the students sat to hear the lecturers in this street of colleges. Dante, in his Paradiso, recalled it as a street illuminated by its teachers. [8] The Rue de la Huchette, for
seven centuries one of the most noted streets in Paris, wan-
ders into the square in front of the Saint-Julien-le-Pauvre,
which offers a magnificent view of Notre Dame Cathedral just

across the Seine. The name of this street derives from À
la Huchette d'Or, or Golden Bin, the sign for a thirteenth-
century inn whose doors did not close until well into the
eighteenth century.[9] Along the Huchette is the street now
called the Xavier-Privas, named in the thirties for a popular poet, which street in the seventeenth century was called
the Rue Zacharie. "Zacharie" is not the name of a person
but is a corruption of the fourteenth-century "Saqualie,"
which had been corrupted in the thirteenth century from
"Sac-à-Lie," referring to the lee sacks or wine lees used
by the parchmentmakers of the neighborhood for treating
skins.[10] The Rue Saint-Jacques, an old Roman road, led
from Notre Dame Cathedral to the left bank. In the Latin
Quarter, most of the bookshops during the manuscript period
were located on this street. The Rue Saint-Jacques was destined to be the haven of printers for centuries to come, for
the places selected by the early manuscript dealers later became the center of the Parisian trade in printed books.[11]

All the street names of Paris, not only those which
show traces of the medieval publishing industry, have meaning. They honor someone or something specific, or they
identify the street by its most prominent medieval shop sign,
or they explain what goes on in that particular street.[12]
That these street names should have survived in spite of the
introduction of new techniques of book production is an in-
teresting phenomenon, because the names were kept alive
for centuries only by word of mouth among a shifting urban
population. There were no street-name signs in Paris until
1729, and for permanence these were marked on stone and
set into the walls of corner buildings where they are still
legible on hundreds of streets.[13] This centuries-old tradition testifies to the strong impression the manuscript publishing industry made upon the people. Pottinger observed
that even the law did not recognize the new techniques and
continued to speak of copyists, illuminators, binders and
others, and not until 1571 did they use the word "printer,"
a whole century after printing was introduced into Paris.[14]

As early as the thirteenth century, the publishing industry had earned for Paris its reputation as "the town of
books," a reference made by Pope Gregory IX in a papal
bull dated 1231.[15] Traces of this renown remain in the
bookstalls found along the river. Here too the present is
blended with the past. It is the city which unites times
present and times past, for sometimes the structures of the
city outlast the functions and purposes that originally brought

them into being, adapting them to new uses.[16] Where the
Seine divides about the ancient section of Paris, the Ile de
la Cité and the Ile Saint-Louis, their quays and those of the
adjacent and immediately westerly banks which had once
been lined with the shops of goldsmiths, watchmakers, and
other craftsmen, have in general been taken over by traders
or booksellers. The parapets of the river walls are occupied by boxes for second-hand books, paintings, and prints,
and their tree-lined walks form a pleasant locality for the
bibliophile.[17] Large bookstores are also found on the boulevard Saint Michel, the main street in the youth of many important Frenchmen while students at the University of Paris,
and where this street meets the boulevard Saint Germain
stands one of the oldest monuments in Paris. Behind the
high brick arches of the Roman baths built about A.D. 200
on the Rue de Cluny is the Cluny Museum, built in 1485 as
a Paris residence for the abbots of Cluny in Burgundy. Here
are housed the Museum's prize possessions, the famous Uni-
corn tapestries.[18] Across the Seine on the Ile de la Cité,
bookstalls are found in the vicinity of Notre Dame Cathedral
near the parvis, once the campus of the Cathedral School of
Notre Dame where the University of Paris began.[19] In the
earlier Middle Ages the cathedral itself took the place of
books. For the unlettered, who had neither psalter, nor
missal, nor the Golden Legend of Jacobus de Voragine, the
cathedral with its sculptured portals and stained glass windows was a book of stone; for the lettered, its western façade was a summa of encyclopedic teaching.[20] This people's
book of stone was gradually rendered obsolete by the coming
of the printed book.

      For almost seven hundred years, this University
Quarter on the left bank was a city within a city with its
own language, its own law, its own sovereign authority.
The language was Latin and remained so until the Revolution; the law, that of the Church; the authority, that of the
University of Paris, which recognized only the Pope of Rome
as its superior.[21] The development of the publishing industry before and after the introduction of printing into Paris
was shaped by this reality.

Expansion of the City

      For three centuries the development of Paris was
tightly contained within the thirteenth-century walls of Philip
II Augustus. During the reign of King Francis I, who ruled

from 1515 to 1547, the city of Paris increased in size and
began to be adorned with buildings in the Renaissance style,
the Hotel de Ville being an example.[22] A huge detailed
tapestry map made by craftsmen to deck the front of the
new Hotel de Ville, whose public square had been the chosen
stage for great historical pageantry on days of public ceremony, illustrates the Paris of Francis I. The Cité of 1540
is covered with important public buildings; the left bank is
studded with colleges, with religious houses, with churches,
with picturesquely named streets where trades are plied.[23]
In 1524 the city contained about three hundred and fifty thousand people, while the University of Paris, although it had
declined, still numbered about ten thousand students during
the reign of Francis I.[24] The energy of Paris which had
been compressed within the city wall broke through this wall
in response to the pressure of city growth and was conveyed
into the suburbs. The need for a new enclosing wall made
itself felt. Although the lines of this wall were laid down in
the sixteenth century, the wall itself was not built until the
reign of Louis XIII (1601-1643), and then only on the right
bank.[25] By the end of the sixteenth century, the population
of Paris had grown to approximately four hundred thousand
inhabitants, an increase of about fifty thousand.[26] Coryat,
writing in 1608, observed that the Rue Saint-Jacques was
"very full of booksellers that have faire shoppes most plenti-
fully furnished with bookes."[27] Paris at the end of the sixteenth century was still, according to Coryat, a town of books.

Notes

1. Jean Porcher, Medieval French Miniatures (New York:
    Harry N. Abrams, Inc., 1959), p. 44.

2. Putnam, op. cit., I, 262.

3. Lehmann-Haupt, op. cit., p. 11.

4. Putnam, op. cit., I, 217.

5. Renard, op. cit., p. 2.

6. Laffont, op. cit., p. 49.

7. Ehrlich, op. cit., p. 141.

8. Ibid.

9. Ibid., p. 143.

10. Ibid.

11. Putnam, op. cit., I, 262.

12. Ehrlich, op. cit., p. 85.

13. Ibid.

14. Pottinger, op. cit., p. 118.

15. Mâle, op. cit., p. 83.

16. Mumford, op. cit., p. 98.

17. "Paris," op. cit., p. 291.

18. Ehrlich, op. cit., p. 144.

19. Ibid., p. 180.

20. Mâle, op. cit., p. 23.

21. Ehrlich, op. cit., pp. 132-33.

22. "Paris," op. cit., p. 289.

23. Laffont, op. cit., p. 28.

24. Putnam, op. cit., II, 28.

25. "Paris," op. cit., p. 289.

26. Putnam, op. cit., II, 95.

27. Ibid.

Chapter 9

SUMMARY

The period of expansion of the city of Paris and the period of the golden age of typography in the first half of the sixteenth century coincide roughly with the reign of Francis I. The fortunes of Paris were closely bound up with those of the French monarchy. A summary of the reign of Francis I, therefore, presents the happenings in Paris as they affected the design of the city and the production of books.

The reign of Francis I summarized the accomplishments of his predecessors and brought them to a peak of achievement which made his reign an exceptionally spectacular one: the progress of royal absolutism, the Italian campaigns, the flowering of Humanism, the encouragement of book production and printing. All of these achievements assured the renown of a prince whom a particularly careful education had polished. It was also in the reign of Francis I that Protestantism was introduced into Paris and the royal authority made its first efforts to stamp it out. Each of the forces of Bourgeoisie, University, Church, which were then dominant in Paris, felt the influence of the force of the Monarchy.

To Francis I it was important to maintain and enhance the prestige of the monarchy. He considerably strengthened royal authority; without the achievement of Francis I in this sphere the absolute monarchy of Louis XIV could never have evolved.[1] The Louvre, originally constructed as a fortress by Philip II Augustus, was transformed into a palace by Francis I.[2]

King Francis recognized the importance of the bourgeoisie to the welfare of the State. In continuous need of loans from the merchant bankers for his conquest of Italy, Francis I founded the port of Le Havre in 1517 at the mouth of the Seine, its plan a characteristic portus layout with strong emphasis on access streets and quays.[3]

Francis I showed an intelligent appreciation of the importance of the development of learning and literature as well for the prestige of the monarchy as for the welfare of the State, and the role of printing in that development. He was the only European ruler of the time who gave any important cooperation to the encouragement of literature and the development of the still new art of printing.[4] The campaigns of Francis I in Italy had brought to Paris a realization of the highest ideals of Renaissance scholarship. King of the French Renaissance, Francis I was a patron of arts and letters. He attracted to France and installed at Fontainebleau, the royal residence, a large number of Italian painters and sculptors, among them Benvenuto Cellini and Leonardo da Vinci.[5] Paris as the center of the brilliant court of Francis I attained pre-eminence in art and literature. The support that the king gave to Humanism was significant. At the University of Paris, education founded essentially on the scholastic method had become rigidly fixed, and as a result the university made little contribution to the Humanism of the Renaissance.[6] King Francis, on the contrary, patronized humanists and subsidized the "new learning." Francis I founded the Collège de France in 1530 at the request of the renowned scholar Guillaume Budé. He made certain that the lecteurs royaux in Hebrew, in Greek, in Latin, and after 1539 in medicine and mathematics, were completely independent of the reactionary Sorbonne. However, although he always encouraged humanists, after 1534 he became more cautious with them.[7]

At Fontainebleau, Francis I imitated the Medici in book collecting, for he had a personal interest in books and in printing. He took pleasure in inspecting the work of the printers, and as a bibliophile, he set the fashion of forming libraries of handsomely printed and choicely bound books.[8] The most famous of these collectors was Jean Grolier, a name famous even today for artistic bookmaking. Grolier, for some years Ambassador of France at Rome, had a personal library said to have contained no less than three thousand volumes.[9]

Francis I continued the work of a predecessor, Charles V, who is considered to be the real founder of the Royal Library, now the Bibliothèque Nationale, by introducing in 1537 the compulsory deposit of books.[10] An edict dated 1537 was the earliest example in France of securing for the printers an authorization for the publication of a book, a concession which was not yet a copyright and not always even a privilege, in consideration of a tax imposed for the benefit of the nation, this tax comprising a single copy of the work authorized. [11] The reason given for the collection in the Royal Library of copies of all works issued in France or imported into the kingdom was the importance of preserving for future generations valuable literature which might otherwise have disappeared altogether from the memory of man, or which might in later issues have been altered from the original and accurate text. [12] This edict, therefore, may be considered as the first step toward the formation of a library for the preservation of the national literature. [13] The collections of the Bibliothèque Nationale today cover every field of human endeavor. Francis I also installed the office of Librarian to the King, a post first held by the aforementioned scholar Guillaume Budé. [14]

The work of the scholarly printer-publishers was held in high esteem by King Francis, and he was prepared to further this work with the royal protection, with privileges, and at times with direct financial aid. [15] In most cases he was ready to throw the influence of the Crown upon the side of a liberal standard of supervision for the productions of the Paris press. The most important service of this king to the printer-publishers had been to use his influence in protecting them against the doctors of the Sorbonne. The experience of Robert Estienne is representative.

The title of "Printer in Greek to the King" had been given to Robert Estienne in 1540 with the special purpose of securing for him an additional safeguard against the attacks of the theological censors. [16] Official recognition and approval by the Crown of his undertakings could not, however, save them from the censure of the Sorbonne. Various rigorous proceedings were instituted against him. On one occasion, Robert Estienne, upon publication of a work considered to be controversial, was suspect and was compelled to flee to the king's court for safety. [17] The untimely death of Francis I at the age of fifty-three was a serious misfortune to Robert Estienne personally and to the cause of liberal scholarship and literary production in general. Robert Estienne found that the policy of the new king, Henry II, was certain to vacillate from month to month according to the personal, political, or ecclesiastical influences which might be brought to bear. Since he was not prepared to discontinue his scholarly publishing undertakings, Robert Estienne transferred his business to Geneva in 1552. [18] Not without reason did Robert Estienne adopt as his device a spreading

olive tree with some branches broken off, and the motto
Noli altum sapere, sed time, based upon Romans 11:20, "Be
not high-minded, but fear."[19] His life, however, contradicted
his printer's device, for he was high-minded and at least he
refused to be fearful.

The situation described above, in which a nation's
most outstanding publisher found it necessary to seek refuge
at the court of the king in order to protect himself against
the violence of officials who were that king's censors, at
least technically, points up the strength and the weakness of
the monarchy. Although Francis I had all the authority of
the kingdom at his command, he was evidently unable to put
any restriction upon the operations of the ecclesiastical censors. The Sorbonne doctors, on the other hand, although
backed by the full authority of the Church of Rome, were
not strong enough to put a stop to publications which they
deemed to be dangerously heretical.[20] This situation also
signifies the disharmony among the forces dominant in the
city of Paris which challenged the medieval order. The
close harmony that had prevailed among the forces of Monarchy, Church, University, and Bourgeoisie, which had been
the primary factor in promoting the greatness of Paris in its
Golden Age of the thirteenth century, had by the sixteenth
seriously degenerated. Each of these forces had entered
upon a period of strain, and the effects were apparent in
the decline of Paris in the latter half of the sixteenth century and the decline in both the quantity and quality of book
production. Francis I had been overpowered by the spirit
of the time. Yet no other monarch had done so much for
scholarly literature as Francis I,[21] and his achievement left
its abiding mark upon book production and upon the city of
Paris.

Although Paris experienced a prolonged period of un-
rest and warfare, the seventeenth century brought with it
steadily increasing political power which rose to its height
with the reign of Louis XIV. The University of Paris renewed its fame as one of the most distinguished scientific
and intellectual centers throughout the world and the premier
university of France. With the renewed glory of the city of
Paris and its university, the arts of the book flourished as
never before.[22]

Notes

1. Robert Mandrou, "Francis I, " Encyclopaedia Britannica (1964 ed.), IX, 783.

2. "Paris, " op. cit., p. 293.

3. Moholy-Nagy, op. cit., pp. 214-15.

4. Putnam, op. cit., II, 43.

5. Mandrou, op. cit., p. 783.

6. Pacaut, op. cit., p. 305.

7. Mandrou, op. cit., p. 783.

8. Putnam, op. cit., II, 43.

9. Ibid.

10. Svend Dahl, History of the Book (New York: The Scarecrow Press, Inc., 1958), p. 70.

11. Putnam, op. cit., II, 447.

12. Ibid.

13. Ibid.

14. Ibid., p. 43.

15. Ibid., p. 14.

16. Ibid., p. 38.

17. Ibid., p. 34.

18. Ibid., p. 50.

19. Ibid., pp. 30-31.

20. Ibid., pp. 34-35.

21. Ibid., p. 7.

22. Bland, op. cit., p. 166.

Chapter 10

CULTURAL ROLE OF THE CITY

The role of Paris as a university city in effecting
cultural change in that phase of its history covered in this
study was to create original modes of thought that had authority beyond and in conflict with the old culture.[1] Since
the amount of experience which can be achieved by direct
effort within a single lifetime is limited, man's capability
depends upon his having access to remoter events, remembered or projected, and to remote or inaccessible parts of
his environment.[2] The city of Paris met the needs of its
society by providing an environment widened in space and
time which was conducive to cultural change by adequately
performing its functions of cultural storage, creative addition to culture, and the dissemination and interchange of
culture. By means of storage facilities such as secular
buildings, sacred buildings, vaults; through symbolic
methods of storage such as manuscripts, books, tapestries,
stained glass windows, sculpture; and through the development of forms such as the archive, the library and the university, the city of Paris became capable of performing its
most essential role as a university city: that of enlarging
and transmitting a complex culture from generation to generation. Through its monuments, written records, and orderly habits of association, the city of Paris enlarged the
scope of all human activities, extending them backward and
forward in time. The city gathered together not only the
physical means, but the human agents needed to pass on and
to enlarge this heritage.[3] Within the environment thus
created, religious, philosophical, and literary specialists
synthesized and created out of the traditional material new
arrangements and developments which were felt to be out-
growths of the old. Through its concentration of physical
and cultural power, the city of Paris heightened the tempo
of the human dialogue; and through the prestige it attained
as a capital city, it widened the circle of those participating
in that dialogue. The physical form of Paris as a walled

174

island city accelerated the tempo of cultural change. The city of Paris became a catalyst for religious and intellectual ferment, and the University of Paris developed within this urban cultural milieu.

The University of Paris, by attracting and bringing together all the talents within its walls, following the pattern of the city, became the center for the production, exchange, and competition of ideas, and created an environment capable of molding new personalities. To this institution came free-lance teachers and freelance students absorbed with a passion for exploring knowledge, prepared to analyze and resolve the persistent problems of Western thought: the nature of the world, of man, of the deity, and the relations between them. Their restless intellectual quest shattered the framework of the old cultural pattern. The typical intellectual dialogue was no longer limited to a dialogue of the soul with God within the framework of authority; it now became also a dia-logue of one thinker with another, arguing debatable points within the framework of logic, using the new intellectual tools of dialectic. [4] The human catalyst who generated the change was Abelard, an urban man. The functions per-formed by Paris, the university city, of cultural storage, creative addition to culture, and the dissemination and inter-change of culture, were now being adequately performed by the University of Paris in its own way. In this connection the University of Paris made explicit in its own right as a secular function one of the necessary activities of the city of Paris: the withdrawal from immediate practical responsi-bilities and the critical reappraisal and renewal of the cul-tural heritage through the direct intercommunication between master and student. In performing these functions, the Uni-versity of Paris assumed the city's cultural role of enlarg-ing and transmitting the intellectual heritage. To paraphrase Mumford, without the agency of the university, with its long memory, its disciplined devotion to intellectual communica-tion and cooperation, the enlargement and transmission of the intellectual heritage would have been inconceivable on the scale actually achieved since the thirteenth century. [5]

Notes

1.   The argument on the cultural role of Paris is based upon a scheme of constructs presented by Robert Redfield and Milton B. Singer in their article en-titled "The Cultural Role of Cities," Economic De-

velopment and Cultural Change, III (1954), 53-73.
The responsibility for the application of these constructs is the writer's.

2. Mumford, op. cit., p. 112.

3. Based upon a concept presented by Mumford, op. cit.,
    p. 569. The writer assumes the responsibility for
    the application of this concept.

4. Morrall, op. cit., p. 136.

5. Mumford, op. cit., p. 276.

BIBLIOGRAPHY

Adams, Henry. Mont-Saint-Michel and Chartres. New York: The Heritage Press, 1933. 348 pp.

Artz, Frederick B. The Mind of the Middle Ages. Third edition revised. New York: Alfred A. Knopf, Inc., 1965. 572 pp.

Aston, Margaret. The Fifteenth Century. New York: Harcourt, Brace and World, Inc., 1968. 216 pp.

Barker, Ernest. "Aristotle," Encyclopaedia Britannica (1964 ed.), II, 391-96.

Bland, David. A History of Book Illustration. Berkeley, California: University of California Press, 1969. 459 pp.

Burton, William Henry. "Methods of Teaching," Encyclopaedia Britannica (1964 ed.), XXI, 866B-67.

Buytaert, Eligius M. "William of Occam," Encyclopaedia Britannica (1964 ed.), XVI, 680-81.

Cantor, Norman F. Medieval History. New York: The Macmillan Company, 1963. 622 pp.

Clark, George. Early Modern Europe. New York: Oxford University Press (A Galaxy Book), 1960. 261 pp.

Crump, C. G., and E. F. Jacob. The Legacy of the Middle Ages. Oxford: The Clarendon Press, 1948. 548 pp.

Dahl, Svend. History of the Book. New York: The Scarecrow Press, Inc., 1958. 279 pp.

Douglas, David. "The Paris of Abelard and St. Louis," Cities of Destiny, Arnold Toynbee, editor. New York:

McGraw-Hill Book Company, 1967. pp. 178-193.

Ehrlich, Blake. Paris on the Seine. New York: Atheneum,
    1962. 375 pp.

Evans, Joan. Life in Medieval France. Revised edition.
    London: Phaidon Press, 1957. 254 pp.

Findlay, John Niemeyer. "Dialectic, " Encyclopaedia Britan-
    nica (1964 ed.), VII 356-57.

Fleming, William. Arts and Ideas. Third edition. New
    York: Holt, Rinehart and Winston, Inc. , 1968. 580 pp.

Fletcher, Banister. A History of Architecture on the Com-
    parative Method. Sixteenth edition. New York: Charles
    Scribner's Sons, 1958. 1033 pp.

"France, " Encyclopaedia Britannica (1964 ed.), IX, 686-776.

"Francis Bacon, " Encyclopaedia Britannica (1964 ed.), II,
    993-99.

Frankl, Paul. "Gothic Architecture, " Encyclopaedia Britan-
    nica (1964 ed.), X, 597-605.

Fremantle, Anne, and others. Age of Faith. (Great Ages
    of Man Series.) New York: Time Incorporated, 1965.
    192 pp.

Gardner, Helen. Art Through the Ages. Fourth edition.
    New York: Harcourt, Brace and Company, 1959.
    840 pp.

Genicot, Leopold. Contours of the Middle Ages. London:
    Routledge and Kegan Paul, 1967. 322 pp.

Gies, Joseph, and Frances Gies. Life in a Medieval City.
    New York: Thomas Y. Crowell Company, 1969.
    274 pp.

Gombrich, E. H. The Story of Art. New York: Phaidon
    Publishers, Inc. , 1951. 462 pp.

Guérard, Albert Léon. French Civilization. New York:
    Cooper Square Publishers, Inc. , 1969. 328 pp.

Haebler, Konrad.   The Study of Incunabula.   Trans., Lucy
     Eugenia Osborne.   New York: The Grolier Club, 1933.
     241 pp.

Hay, Denys.   "Fiat Lux, " Printing and the Mind of Man,
     John Carter and others, editors.   New York: Holt,
     Rinehart and Winston, 1967.   Pp. xv-xxx.

"History of Education, " Encyclopaedia Britannica (1964 ed.),
     VII, 982-1015.

Hodgen, Margaret T.   Change and History.   (Viking Fund
     Publications in Anthropology No. 18.)   New York:
     Wenner-Gren Foundation for Anthropological Research,
     Inc., 1952.   324 pp.

Hofer, Philip.   "The Illustration of Books, " A History of the
     Printed Book, Lawrence C. Wroth, editor.   New York:
     The Limited Editions Club, 1938.   Pp. 389-421.

Hohler, Christopher.   "Court Life in Peace and War, " The
     Flowering of the Middle Ages, Joan Evans, editor.
     New York: McGraw-Hill Book Company, 1966.   Pp.
     134-178.

Hunt, Richard.   "Universities and Learning, " The Flowering
     of the Middle Ages, Joan Evans, editor.   New York:
     McGraw-Hill Book Company, 1966.   Pp. 180-202.

Huyghe, Rene.   "Art Forms and Society, " Larousse Encyclo-
     pedia of Byzantine and Medieval Art, pp. 313-22.   New
     York: Prometheus Press, 1963.

Johnson, A. F.   "The Sixteenth Century, " A History of the
     Printed Book, Lawrence C. Wroth, editor.   New York:
     The Limited Editions Club, 1938.   Pp. 121-55.

Johnson, Elmer D.   A History of Libraries in the Western
     World.   New York: The Scarecrow Press, Inc., 1965.
     418 pp.

Kilham, Walter Harrington.   "Library Architecture, " Encyclo-
     paedia Britannica (1964 ed.), XIV, 25-28.

King, Donald.   "Industry, Merchants and Money, " The
     Flowering of the Middle Ages, Joan Evans, editor.
     New York: McGraw-Hill Book Company, 1966.

Pp. 246-80.

Kneale, William Calvert. "Scientific Method, " Encyclopaedia
     Britannica (1964 ed.), XX, 126-29.

Laffont, Robert (ed.). The Illustrated History of Paris and
     the Parisians. Garden City, New York: Doubleday
     and Company, 1958. 292 pp.

Lehmann-Haupt, Hellmut. Peter Schoeffer of Gernsheim and
     Mainz. New York: The Printing House of Leo Hart,
     1950. 146 pp.

"Louis IX, " Encyclopaedia Britannica (1964 ed.), XIV, 415-16.

McLuhan, Marshall. The Gutenberg Galaxy. Toronto: Uni-
     versity of Toronto Press, 1965. 293 pp.

McMurtrie, Douglas C. The Book. Third revised edition.
     New York: Oxford University Press, 1943. 676 pp.

Mâle, Emile. The Gothic Image. Trans., Dora Nussey.
     New York: Harper and Row (Harper Torchbook), 1958.
     414 pp.

Mandrou, Robert. "Francis I, " Encyclopaedia Britannica
     (1964 ed.), IX, 782-83.

Meiss, Millard. "Preface, " The Très Riches Heures of
     Jean, Duke of Berry. Reproduced from the illuminated
     manuscript. New York: George Braziller, 1969.
     Pp. 7-12.

Merryweather, F. Somner. Bibliomania in the Middle Ages.
     London: The Woodstock Press, 1933. 288 pp.

Miller, William. "Publishing, " Encyclopaedia Britannica
     (1964 ed.), XVIII, 749-52.

Minio-Paluello, Lorenzo. "Peter Abelard, " Encyclopaedia
     Britannica (1964 ed.), I, 26-27.

Mitchell, Ann. Cathedrals of Europe. (Great Buildings of
     the World Series.) Feltham, Middlesex: Paul Hamlyn,
     1968. 189 pp.

Moholy-Nagy, Sibyl. Matrix of Man. New York: Frederick

A. Praeger, 1968. 317 pp.

Morrall, John B. The Medieval Imprint. New York: Basic
    Books, Inc., 1967. 156 pp.

Mortet, Charles. "France," Printing: A Short History of
    the Art, R. A. Peddie, editor. London: Grafton and
    Company, 1927. Pp. 63-88.

Mumford, Lewis. The City in History. New York: Har-
    court, Brace and World, Inc., 1961. 657 pp.

Oldenbourg, Zoe. "With Stone and Faith," The Horizon
    Book of Great Cathedrals, Jay Jacobs, editor. New
    York: American Heritage Publishing Company, Inc.,
    1968. Pp. 7-25.

Pacaut, Marcel Pierre. "Paris University," Encyclopaedia
    Britannica (1964 ed.), XVII, 304-5.

Palmer, R. R., and Joel Colton. A History of the Modern
    World. Second edition. New York: Alfred A. Knopf,
    Inc., 1956. 945 pp.

"Paris," Encyclopaedia Britannica (1964 ed.), XVII, 285-97.

Pears, David Francis. "Nominalism," Encyclopaedia Britan-
    nica (1964 ed.), XVI, 482.

"Philip II," Encyclopaedia Britannica (1964 ed.), XVII, 720-
    21.

Porcher, Jean. Medieval French Miniatures. New York:
    Harry N. Abrams, Inc. 1959. 275 pp.

Pottinger, David T. The French Book Trade in the Ancien
    Regime: 1500-1791. Cambridge, Mass.: Harvard
    University Press, 1958. 363 pp.

Powicke, F. M. Ways of Medieval Life and Thought. Bos-
    ton: The Beacon Press, 1951. 255 pp.

"Printing," Encyclopaedia Britannica (1964 ed.), XVIII, 500-
    505.

Putnam, George Haven. Books and Their Makers During the
    Middle Ages. 2 vols. New York: Hillary House Pub-

lishers, Ltd., 1962.

Redfield, Robert, and Milton B. Singer. "The Cultural Role of Cities," Economic Development and Cultural Change, III (1954), 53-73.

Reinhardt, Kurt F. Germany, 2000 Years. Revised edition. New York: Frederick Ungar Publishing Company, 1961. 428 pp.

Renard, Georges. Guilds in the Middle Ages. (Reprints of Economic Classics.) New York: Augustus M. Kelley, 1968. 139 pp.

Robb, David M., and J. J. Garrison. Art in the Western World. Third edition. New York: Harper and Brothers, 1953. 1050 pp.

Robinson, James Harvey. Readings in European History. Boston: Ginn and Company, 1904. 551 pp.

Rörig, Fritz. The Medieval Town. Berkeley, California: University of California Press, 1967. 208 pp.

Rothe, Edith. Mediaeval Book Illumination in Europe. New York: W. W. Norton and Company, Inc., 1968. 306 pp.

Saalman, Howard. Medieval Cities. (Planning and Cities Series, ed. George R. Collins.) New York: George Braziller, 1968. 127 pp.

"Scholasticism," Encyclopaedia Britannica (1964 ed.), XX, 81-82.

Simon, Edith, and others. The Reformation. (Great Ages of Man Series.) New York: Time Incorporated, 1966. 191 pp.

Singer, Charles. "Science," Encyclopaedia Britannica (1964 ed.), XX, 114-24.

Southern, R. W. The Making of the Middle Ages. New Haven: Yale University Press, 1961. 280 pp.

Starr, Chester G., and others. A History of the World. 2 vols. Chicago: Rand McNally and Company, 1960.

Stephenson, Carl. Mediaeval History. Third edition. New
    York: Harper and Brothers, 1935. 551 pp.

Temko, Allan. Notre-Dame of Paris. (Time Reading Pro-
    gram special edition.) New York: Time Incorporated,
    1955. 343 pp.

Thompson, James Westfall. The Medieval Library. New
    York: Hafner Publishing Company, 1967. 702 pp.

Thompson, James Westfall, and Edgar Nathaniel Johnson.
    An Introduction to Medieval Europe, 300-1500. New
    York: W. W. Norton and Company, Inc. 1937.
    1092 pp.

Toynbee, Arnold. Cities on the Move. New York: Oxford
    University Press, 1970. 257 pp.

Toynbee, Arnold (ed.). Cities of Destiny. New York:
    McGraw-Hill Book Company, 1967. 376 pp.

Traill, H. D. (ed.). The Capitals of the World. New York:
    Harper and Brothers, 1894. 701 pp.

The Très Riches Heures of Jean, Duke of Berry. Repro-
    duced from the illuminated manuscript. New York:
    George Braziller, 1969. 139 pp.

"Universities," Encyclopaedia Britannica (1964 ed.), XXII,
    862-79.

Winger, Howard Woodrow. "Book," Encyclopaedia Britannica
    (1964 ed.), III, 919-29.

Wood, Charles T. The Age of Chivalry. New York: Uni-
    verse Books, 1970. 175 pp.

INDEX